Copyright © 2021 by

I0015190

DOMAIN 1: SECURITY AND RISK MANAGEMENT (15%) 5

1.1 UNDERSTAND, ADHERE TO, AND PROMOTE PROFESSIONAL ETHICS 5
1.2 UNDERSTAND AND APPLY SECURITY CONCEPTS 5
1.3 EVALUATE AND APPLY SECURITY GOVERNANCE PRINCIPLES 6
1.4 DETERMINE COMPLIANCE AND OTHER REQUIREMENTS 10
1.5 UNDERSTAND LEGAL AND REGULATORY ISSUES THAT PERTAIN TO
INFORMATION SECURITY IN A HOLISTIC CONTEXT 13
1.6 UNDERSTAND REQUIREMENTS FOR INVESTIGATION TYPES (I.E.,
ADMINISTRATIVE, CRIMINAL, CIVIL, REGULATORY, INDUSTRY STANDARDS) 16
1.7 DEVELOP, DOCUMENT, AND IMPLEMENT SECURITY POLICY, STANDARDS,
PROCEDURES, AND GUIDELINES 17
1.8 IDENTIFY, ANALYZE, AND PRIORITIZE BUSINESS CONTINUITY (BC)
REQUIREMENTS 18
1.9 CONTRIBUTE TO AND ENFORCE PERSONNEL SECURITY POLICIES AND
PROCEDURES 18
1.10 UNDERSTAND AND APPLY RISK MANAGEMENT CONCEPTS 20
1.11 UNDERSTAND AND APPLY THREAT MODELING CONCEPTS AND
METHODOLOGIES 28
1.12 APPLY SUPPLY CHAIN RISK MANAGEMENT (SCRM) CONCEPTS 29
1.13 ESTABLISH AND MAINTAIN A SECURITY AWARENESS, EDUCATION, AND
TRAINING PROGRAM 32
TERMS AND DEFINITIONS: 33

DOMAIN 2: ASSET SECURITY (10%) 35

2.1 IDENTIFY AND CLASSIFY INFORMATION AND ASSETS 35
2.2 ESTABLISH INFORMATION AND ASSET HANDLING REQUIREMENTS 35
2.3   PROVISION RESOURCES SECURELY 36
2.4 MANAGE DATA LIFECYCLE 37
2.5 ENSURE APPROPRIATE ASSET RETENTION 39
2.6 DETERMINE DATA SECURITY CONTROLS AND COMPLIANCE REQUIREMENTS . 40

DOMAIN 3: SECURITY ARCHITECTURE AND ENGINEERING (13%) 42

3.1 RESEARCH, IMPLEMENT AND MANAGE ENGINEERING PROCESSES USING
SECURE DESIGN PRINCIPLES 42
3.2 UNDERSTAND THE FUNDAMENTAL CONCEPTS OF SECURITY MODELS 45
3.3 SELECT CONTROLS BASED UPON SYSTEMS SECURITY REQUIREMENTS 48
3.4 UNDERSTAND SECURITY CAPABILITIES OF INFORMATION SYSTEMS (IS) 49

3.5 ASSESS AND MITIGATE THE VULNERABILITIES OF SECURITY ARCHITECTURES, DESIGNS, AND SOLUTION ELEMENTS 54

3.6 SELECT AND DETERMINE CRYPTOGRAPHIC SOLUTIONS............................ 58

3.7 UNDERSTAND METHODS OF CRYPTANALYTIC ATTACKS 64

3.8 APPLY SECURITY PRINCIPLES TO SITE AND FACILITY DESIGN 67

3.9 DESIGN SITE AND FACILITY SECURITY CONTROLS.................................... 69

DOMAIN 4: COMMUNICATION AND NETWORK SECURITY (13%) **76**

4.1 ASSESS AND IMPLEMENT SECURE DESIGN PRINCIPLES IN NETWORK ARCHITECTURES.. 76

4.2 SECURE NETWORK COMPONENTS.. 91

4.3 IMPLEMENT SECURE COMMUNICATION CHANNELS ACCORDING TO DESIGN . 93

DOMAIN 5: IDENTITY AND ACCESS MANAGEMENT (IAM) (13%) **99**

5.1 CONTROL PHYSICAL AND LOGICAL ACCESS TO ASSETS 99

5.2 MANAGE IDENTIFICATION AND AUTHENTICATION OF PEOPLE, DEVICES, AND SERVICES... 101

5.3 FEDERATED IDENTITY WITH A THIRD-PARTY SERVICE 104

5.4 IMPLEMENT AND MANAGE AUTHORIZATION MECHANISMS 105

5.5 MANAGE THE IDENTITY AND ACCESS PROVISIONING LIFECYCLE 106

5.6 IMPLEMENT AUTHENTICATION SYSTEMS 108

DOMAIN 6: SECURITY TESTING AND ASSESSMENT (12%) **112**

6.1 DESIGN AND VALIDATE ASSESSMENT, TEST, AND AUDIT STRATEGIES......... 112

6.2 CONDUCT SECURITY CONTROL TESTING 113

6.3 COLLECT SECURITY PROCESS DATA (E.G., TECHNICAL AND ADMINISTRATIVE) 117

6.4 ANALYZE TEST OUTPUT AND GENERATE REPORT 120

6.5 CONDUCT OR FACILITATE SECURITY AUDITS 121

DOMAIN 7: SECURITY OPERATIONS (13%) **123**

7.1 UNDERSTAND AND COMPLY WITH INVESTIGATIONS.............................. 123

7.2 CONDUCT LOGGING AND MONITORING ACTIVITIES.............................. 126

7.3 PERFORM CONFIGURATION MANAGEMENT (CM) (E.G., PROVISIONING, BASELINING, AUTOMATION).. 128

7.4 APPLY FOUNDATIONAL SECURITY OPERATIONS CONCEPTS...................... 129

7.5 APPLY RESOURCE PROTECTION.. 130

7.6 CONDUCT INCIDENT MANAGEMENT 132

7.7 OPERATE AND MAINTAIN DETECTIVE AND PREVENTATIVE MEASURES 133

7.8 IMPLEMENT AND SUPPORT PATCH AND VULNERABILITY MANAGEMENT 136

7.9 UNDERSTAND AND PARTICIPATE IN CHANGE MANAGEMENT PROCESSES ... 137

7.10 IMPLEMENT RECOVERY STRATEGIES 138

7.11 IMPLEMENT DISASTER RECOVERY (DR) PROCESSES 139

7.12 TEST DISASTER RECOVERY PLANS (DRP) 141

7.13 PARTICIPATE IN BUSINESS CONTINUITY (BC) PLANNING AND EXERCISES . 142

7.14 IMPLEMENT AND MANAGE PHYSICAL SECURITY.................................. 143

7.15 ADDRESS PERSONNEL SAFETY AND SECURITY CONCERNS...................... 144

DOMAIN 8: SOFTWARE DEVELOPMENT (11%) 146

8.1 UNDERSTAND AND INTEGRATE SECURITY IN THE SOFTWARE DEVELOPMENT LIFE CYCLE (SDLC) 146

8.2 IDENTIFY AND APPLY SECURITY CONTROLS IN SOFTWARE DEVELOPMENT ECOSYSTEMS.. 149

8.3 ASSESS THE EFFECTIVENESS OF SOFTWARE SECURITY 152

8.4 ASSESS SECURITY IMPACT OF ACQUIRED SOFTWARE 153

8.5 DEFINE AND APPLY SECURE CODING GUIDELINES AND STANDARDS........... 155

DOMAIN 1: Security and Risk Management (15%)

1.1 Understand, adhere to, and promote professional ethics

ISC2 Code of Ethics:

1. Protect society, the common good, necessary public trust and confidence, and the infrastructure
2. Act honorable, honestly, justly, responsible, and legally
3. Provide diligent and competent service to principals
4. Advance and protect the profession

*Can lose certification for violation

1.2 Understand and apply security concepts

Confidentiality: protecting personal privacy and proprietary information

Integrity: data is protected from unauthorized changes to ensure that it is reliable and correct

Availability: Ensuring timely and reliable access to and use of information by authorized users.

Authenticity: The ability to ensure that the information originates or is endorsed from the source which is attributed to that information

Nonrepudiation: Inability to deny.

1.3 Evaluate and apply security governance principles

Alignment of the security function to business

Mission Statement: explains company culture, values, ethics, core goals, and agenda.

Business Strategy: an organization long term goals and how it plans to affect them.

Business Goals: objectives that a company expects to achieve within a specific time frame, typically in the near or short term.

Business Objectives: the defined, measurable results that a company hopes to sustain as it grows.

With each of the above business strategies, mission, goals, and objectives security should be reflected in each to provide a top-down approach towards cyber security for an organization.

Top->Down Approach: Top management directs and supports security.

Bottom->Up Approach: IT department drives the security initiatives and attempts to get top management to approve security measures.

Organizational processes

Board of Directors: An executive body that governs corporate management and set oversight policies of an organization or company, typically elected officials that represent the best interest of the shareholders

Governance Committee: a collection of executives and/or managers who meet on a regular basis to discuss security events, initiatives, operational metrics, and other issues that affect them.

Audit Committee: a subsection of the Board of Directors that is in charge of oversight of financial reporting and disclosure.

Acquisitions: When an entity or company acquires by means of purchase another entity or company. The main security concerns are additional data types that may require more protection, employees, and roles that may not meet security standards. It is also a concern that the acquired company may have existing security vulnerabilities or have an active threat in the network, due diligence should be taken to protect the security of both networks during acquisition process.

Merger: When two entities combine to form a single entity. The main security concerns are additional data types that may require more protection, employees, and roles that may not meet security standards. It is also a concern that one of the origin companies may have existing security vulnerabilities or have active threats in the network. Due diligence should be taken to ensure new networks are secure.

Divestitures: When a portion of a company or subsidiary is sold. The chief concern is the interconnection of IT and security functions and data loss.

Organizational Roles and Responsibilities

Chief Executive Officer (CEO): the highest-ranking person in a company, the CEO oversees a company's or organization's overall success as well as making top-level management choices.

Chief Financial Officer (CFO): a senior executive who oversees a company's financial operations, the CFO's responsibilities include managing cash flow and financial planning, as well as analyzing and proposing remedial actions for the company's financial strengths and shortcomings.

Chief Operating Officer (COO): a top executive in charge of a company's administrative and operational tasks on a day-to-day basis.

Chief Information Officer (CIO): a senior executive of a company who works with information technology and computer systems to help the company achieve its objectives. Sometimes referred to as CTO.

Chief Technology Officer (CTO): a senior executive of a company who works with information technology and computer systems to help the company achieve its objectives. Sometimes referred to as CIO.

Chief Accounting Officer (CAO): a senior executive in charge of accounting for an organization, oversees the monitoring of all accounting functions, ensuring that reporting and bookkeeping are correct and in accordance with the Securities and Exchange Commission's federal rules.

Chief Legal Officer (CLO): the head of the corporate legal department and oversees the company's legal matters, advises the board of

directors, chairman of the board, chief
executive officer, and other senior management
on legal matters.

Data Roles and Responsibilities

Data Owner: determines who has access to
information assets within their functional
areas. A Data Owner can choose to examine and
approve each access request individually, or
they can construct a set of criteria that
govern who is qualified for access based on
business function, support role, and so on.

System Owner: in control of one or more systems
that may include and run data held by multiple
data owners, this is the physical
equipment/networks.

Data Custodian: in charge of the safe custody,
transportation, and storage of data, as well as
the implementation of business regulations.

Data Steward: an oversight or data governance
job within an organization that oversees
verifying the quality and conformance to
requirements of the organization's data assets,
including the metadata for those data assets

User: those utilizing the company systems and
data, should have accepted monitoring policy
and been trained on company policies

Security control frameworks

A security control framework is a well-
organized set of security controls,
implementation, and audit guidelines that
businesses can use as a template or solution to
manage risk.

Due Care and Due Diligence

Due Care: conduct that a reasonable and prudent person with proper training would exercise, careful ongoing operation

Due Diligence: Company properly investigated all its possible weaknesses and vulnerabilities in advance or before an attack

---

1.4 Determine compliance and other requirements

Contractual standards

Payment Card Industry — Data Security Standard (PCI-DSS): a data security guideline for companies that deal with major credit card networks.

Service Organization Control (SOC): reports that aid businesses in building trust and confidence in their service delivery processes and controls.

Legal standards

Federal Information Systems Management Act (FISMA): US laws that provides a set of principles and security standards for the protection of government information systems

Sarbanes-Oxley Act (SOX): Protects investors by increasing corporate responsibility, increased criminal punishment, accounting regulation and new protections.

Industry standards

There are many different standards relating to cybersecurity, risk management and systems security, the *International Organization for Standardization (ISO)* and the *National Institute of Standards and Technology (NIST)* are the two main organizations for standards that we will be looking at. Below are some of the most relevant industry standards, the ones in bold are more likely to show up on a test.

ISO Standards:

- ISO 7498: Open Systems Interconnection (OSI Model)(4.1)
- ISO 17799: Code of Practice
- **ISO 27001: Information Security Management System (1.7)**
- **ISO 27002: Guidance and Best Practices**
- **ISO 27005: Information Security Risk Management**
- ISO 15408: Evaluation Criteria for IT Security (3.3)
- ISO 27006: Guidelines for Audit and Certification(6.1, 6.5)
- ISO 27035: Information Technology
- ISO 27702: Privacy Management System (1.5, 1.9, 3.1)
- **ISO 31000: Risk Management Principles and Guidelines (1.10)**

NIST Standards:

- SP 800-12: Introduction to Information Security
- SP 800-34: Contingency Planning Guide (1.8, 7.11-13)
- **SP 800-37: Risk Management Framework (1.10)**
- **SP 800-53: Security and Privacy Controls (1.5, 1.9, 3.1)**
- SP 800-57: Recommendation for Key Management (3.6)
- SP 800-63-3: Digital Identity Guidelines (5.2, 5.3)
- SP 800-88: Guidelines for Media Sanitization (2.4)
- SP 800-154: Data-Centric Threat Modeling (1.11)
- **SP 800-160: System Security Engineering (3.4-5)**

Regulatory Requirements

General Data Protection Regulation (GDPR): a data protection and privacy rule in EU law for the European Union and the European Economic Area

Federal Acquisition Regulation (FAR): the principal set of rules regarding Government procurement in the United States

Privacy requirements

Health Insurance Portability and Accountability Act (HIPAA): US laws mandating sensitive patient health information is not disclosed without the patient's consent or knowledge.

Article 17 GDPR — Right to erasure: The data subject shall have the right to obtain from the controller the erasure of personal data concerning him or her without undue delay and the controller shall have the obligation to erase personal data without undue delay

Generally Accepted Privacy Principles (GAPP): a framework designed to help Chartered Accountants and Certified Public Accountants develop an efficient privacy program for managing and preventing privacy risks

Waiver of Privacy:
Any reasonable expectation of privacy is waived by your voluntary publication of personal information. (IE social media)

1.5 Understand legal and regulatory issues that pertain to information security in a holistic context

Cybercrimes and data breaches

Cybercrime is defined as a crime in which a computer is either the object of the crime or is utilized as a tool to commit the crime. A cybercriminal may exploit a device to get access to a user's personal information, confidential corporate information, government information, or to deactivate the device. Selling or obtaining the aforementioned information online is likewise criminal.

Art. 33 GDPR - Notification of a personal data breach to the supervisory authority within 72 hours of becoming aware, violation results in 4% of annual global turnover, or 20 million euro, whichever is greater

Import/export controls

Wassenaar Arrangement: formed to promote openness and greater responsibility in the transfer of conventional armaments and dual-use items and technologies to contribute to regional and worldwide security and stability, established 1996, 42 member states.

Symmetric cryptography products of up to 56 bit key length, and asymmetric cryptography products of up to 512 bit key length, are free from export restriction.

The Wassenaar Arrangement includes personal use exemption, allowing for individuals to move freely between countries with personal use cryptography devices, additionally is not binding on the member states.

Licensing and Intellectual Property (IP)

Patents: A patent is a legal right to an invention granted to a person or entity that prevents others from replicating, using, or selling it.US patents last for 20 years

Trademark: a sort of intellectual property that consists of a distinguishable sign, design, or expression that identifies products or service, trademarks used to identify services typically called service marks

Copyrights: a sort of intellectual property that grants the owner the sole right to produce copies of a creative work, US copyrights are valid for 70 years after the author's death.

Trade Secrets: a type of intellectual property consisting of formulas, techniques, processes, designs, instruments, patterns, or information compilations with intrinsic commercial worth

Public Domain: belonging to the public and thus not subject to copyright

Open Source: The original source code is made freely accessible for redistribution and modification.

Freeware: Software that is typically proprietary and is distributed at no monetary cost to the end user.

Per-seat licensing: a software licensing model that is based on the number of individual users that have access to a digital service or product.

Digital Rights Management (DRM): a collection of access control methods used to limit the use of proprietary devices and copyrighted works.

Digital Millennium Copyright Act (DMCA): criminalizes the creation and distribution of technology, devices, or services designed to circumvent restrictions that restrict access to copyrighted material.

Transborder data flow requirements

Organization for Economic Cooperation and Development (OECP): OECD Guidelines on the Protection of Privacy and Transborder Flows of Personal Data, issued in 1980

8 Driving Principals:

1. **Collection Limitation:** collection of personal data should be limited, obtained by lawful and fair means and with knowledge of the subject
2. **Data Quality:** personal data should be kept complete and current, and relevant to the purposes for which it is being used
3. **Purpose Specification:** subjects should be notified of the reason for the collection of their personal information at the time that it is collected, and organization should only use it for the stated purpose
4. **Use Limitation:** only with the consent of the subject or by the authority of law should personal data be disclosed, made available, or used for purposes other than those previously stated
5. **Security Safeguards:** reasonable safeguards should be put in place to protect personal data against risks such as loss, unauthorized access, modification, and disclosure
6. **Openness:** developments, practices, and policies regarding personal data should be openly communicated. In addition, subjects should be able to easily establish the existence of and nature of personal data, its use, and the identity

and usual residence of the organization in possession of that data

7. **Individual Participation:** subject should be able to find out whether an organization has their personal information and what that information is, to correct erroneous data, and to challenge denied requests to do so

8. **Accountability:** organization should be accountable for complying with measures that support the previous principles

Privacy

The right to privacy is a principle under GDPR that states that a subject has the right to be forgotten, or right to erasure. This ultimately means that a person has legal rights to their data and privacy of that data.

Exception to privacy regulations, is when a person submits their own data for public view and consumption, at this point there is no expectation of privacy.

1.6 Understand requirements for investigation types (i.e., administrative, criminal, civil, regulatory, industry standards)

Administrative

This is company policy, administrative regulations and regulations that apply to businesses.

Criminal

Criminal Law: a subset of legal code that defines behavior which is deemed harmful to society and the resulting punishment for violating the legal code results in jail, prison, or death.

Civil

Civil Law: also known as tort law is the law as it relates to contracts, and private obligations, this is law that one party feels another party has wronged them, punishments that are inflicted are financial in nature.

Types of Legal Systems

There are three main types of legal systems that exist, while there are different variations and other systems the main legal systems are Common Law, Legal Code and Religious Law.

Common Law: a body of law that is based on precedent, prior ruling by the courts. A past ruling can be used to influence a judge on how to decide a similar case, this this is also referred to as Case Law.

Legal Code: a body of law that requires the legislature to have an exhaustive set of laws to cover a complete system or particular area.

Religious Law: a body of law that utilizes religious and moral codes to guide the legal system, typically relies upon religious tradition.

1.7 Develop, document, and implement security policy, standards, procedures, and guidelines

Policies: Policies are broad declarations established by a company that define what the company stands for and what its goals are. Effective policies are:

Standards: specified, obligatory standards that define and support higher-level policies

Procedures: a series of steps carried out in a regular and precise order

Guidelines: a general concept, guideline, or piece of guidance that is not enforceable

1.8 Identify, analyze, and prioritize Business Continuity (BC) requirements

Business Impact Analysis (BIA)

Business Impact Analysis (BIA): An examination that identifies the resources vital to an organization's long-term viability as well as the threats to those resources.

Develop and document the scope and the plan

Business continuity (BC) plans should be developed and scoped based on high priority assets and likely threats to the assets. There should be multiple plans that are specific to each of the threats to operations.

Business Continuity (BC): an organizations ability to continue operations in the wake of a disaster and return to normal operations.

1.9 Contribute to and enforce personnel security policies and procedures

Candidate screening and hiring

Candidate Screening: a process should be set that allows for potential hires to have background screening performed prior to onboarding such as credit checks, criminal history check.

Onboarding: a process should be set that indoctrinates new employees and sets expectations, such as signing an NDA, agreeing to the company acceptable use policy and attending a new employee orientation.

Compliance policy requirements

An organization should ensure that they have policies in place that ensure compliance with all federal and state laws and regulations.

Employment agreements and policies

Non-Disclosure Agreement (NDA): a contractual commitment that protected company information shall be kept hidden

Acceptable Use Policy: a policy outlining the restrictions and regulations that a user must accept to have access to a corporate network or the Internet

Privacy policy requirements

Employers should notify employees that they are being monitored, what methods of monitoring are being used, and the consequences for inappropriate use of the systems. Clear workplace policies should be included in awareness training, and users should formally acknowledge that they are subject to those expectations. Consistent execution of those policies should give some protection against selective enforcement.

Onboarding, transfers, and termination processes

Non-Disclosure Agreement (NDA): a contractual commitment that protected company information

shall be kept hidden, should occur during an
onboarding process to protect company
information

Transfers: processes for an internal transfer
should allow a seamless move from one
department to another, while protecting the
security of the company and removing access
that is no longer necessary for the employee.

Termination: processes should be in place to
ensure that accounts are disabled and access
revoked for terminated employees. Additionally,
processes should be in place if the termination
is involuntary to ensure that the employee does
not retaliate in a manner that could cause harm
to the company.

Vendor, consultant, and contractor agreements and controls

Non-Disclosure Agreement (NDA): a contractual
commitment that protected company information
shall be kept hidden, should be signed by any
contractor, vendor or consultant prior to
giving them access to any trade secrets

Service Level Agreement (SLA): agreement
between IT service provider and customer to
guarantee a service or performance level.
Penalties for failure are spelled out in the
contract. An SLA can be utilized to ensure
security level by vendors, consultants, and
contractors.

1.10 Understand and apply risk management concepts

Risk management has four main steps.
1. Identify threats and vulnerabilities
2. Risk Assessment
3. Risk Response

4. Risk Monitoring and Reporting

Identify threats and vulnerabilities

It is the first job of a cybersecurity professional to be able to identify threats and vulnerabilities to the systems that they are protecting.

Threat: Any circumstance or event with the potential to adversely impact organizational operations

Vulnerability: Weakness in an information system, system security procedures, internal controls, or implementation that could be exploited or triggered by a threat.

Threat x Vulnerability = Risk

Risk assessment/analysis

Qualitative Analysis: an approach to assess risk that is intended to be faster than quantitative analysis, this is subjective and conducted based on experience.

- **Risk Matrix:** a matrix that outlines likelihood vs consequence of risk to determine high, medium and low risk.

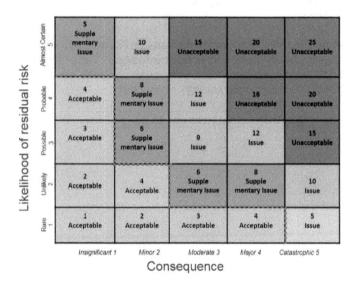

- **Fishbone Diagram:** a type of qualitative analysis also known as a cause and effect diagram, provides a structure to find the root cause of a problem, this is useful in identifying the underlying risk in systems.

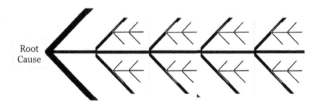

Quantitative Analysis: a numerical approach to identifying risk by using historical data to determine loss expectancy and cost.

- **Asset Value (AV):** The monetary value of any given asset

- **Exposure Factor (EF):** Percentage of loss to a specific asset

- **Single Loss Expectancy (SLE):** Monetary cost of a single successful attack or threat realization **(SLE = AV * EF)**

- **Annual Rate of Occurrence (ARO):** The number of losses that are expected to happen in an average year(s)

- **Annual Loss Expectancy (ALE):** Annual monetary cost that is expected **(ARO * SLE)**

Hybrid Analysis: a hybrid approach will assign numerical values into a subjective matrix, to output a numerical value for a subjective input.

Risk response

There are four main ways to respond to risk:

a. **Risk Avoidance:** Eliminate the risk by avoiding the hazard, activity or technology that exposes you to risk

b. **Risk Transference:** Shift the risk to another entity by means of insurance

c. **Risk Mitigation:** Mitigate risk by preparing for it by reducing exposure and deploying countermeasures.

d. **Risk Acceptance:** Accept the risk and do nothing

Countermeasure selection and implementation

Countermeasure: an action or technology implemented in order to reduce risk or vulnerability to a system

There are many decisions when choosing which countermeasures to implement, some of which are listed below; it is important to ensure that the cost of the countermeasure is not greater than risk itself.

- **Cost:** there can be hidden costs to implementing a countermeasure, such as operating or licenses fees
- **Usability:** what are the effects on productivity, if the security device reduces productivity significantly it is likely not a viable solution
- **Maintenance:** who will maintain the new controls, are additional staff needed, is extra training certification required to staff to maintain the controls
- **Implementation:** what are the requirements to implement the controls, what testing is needed to ensure minimal downtime

Applicable types of controls

There are three categories of controls and seven types of security controls; each of the types will fit into one of the categories. **Security Categories:**

- **Management Controls:** guidance, policies, procedures and instructions for employees to follow, also called administrative controls
- **Operational Controls:** access controls, ACLs, IDS, antivirus, these are also called technical controls
- **Physical Controls:** fences, cameras, security guards these are physical

devices that typically are put in place
as obstacles or barriers to entry

Security Types:

- **Preventative:** intended to block or stop
  malicious actions and damage
- **Detective:** identify malicious actions and
  damage
- **Corrective:** intended to get operations
  back to normal, attempts to correct
  automatically, antivirus, IDS and
  mantraps.
- **Deterrent:** intended to provide a barrier
  to entry by not appearing to be an easy
  target
- **Recovery:** restore system to normal
  operations before attack, more extensive
  than corrective control includes repair
  and backups
- **Compensating:** an alternative solution to
  one that might be cost prohibitive
- **Directive:** extension of management
  control designed to encourage compliance
  with security policies

Control assessments (security and privacy)

Security control assessments are designed
to test the effectiveness of security controls
that have put in place in order to determine
residual risk.

Penetration Testing: penetration tests are an
effective method to test all categories and
types of controls that have been implemented,
this is a broad term and includes social
engineering, phishing, vulnerability assessment
and much more.

Social Engineering: useful for testing
Management, directive and any other controls
that require manipulation of people such as
mantraps.

Monitoring and measurement

It is necessary to implement systems that can monitor and measure the effectiveness of security controls that have been put in place.

Monitoring: the process of collecting and observing activity within a network to assess for threats

Measurement: the process in which the ability to detect an intrusion inside a system is determined

Reporting

Likely one of the most important steps in the risk management process is that of reporting. If senior management does not have a clear understanding of the security assessments and risk calculations that have been conducted, then they will be unable to ensure that the appropriate measures are taken to mitigate risk. Reporting gives management a snapshot view of the effectiveness and condition of the networks in an organization.

Reporting: the process in which findings from controls, assessments and monitoring and measurement are reported to senior management.

Continuous improvement (e.g., Risk maturity modeling)

Risk maturity models are utilized to determine an organizations capability regarding managing and dealing with risk. Once the maturity level of an organization is evaluated, the organization can take the appropriate steps to grow its risk management program. The

process of managing risk is continuous and the
goal of any organization should be to reach the
point that risk management is embedded into
strategic planning and continually being
evaluation and improved.

Maturity Level	Description
Ad hoc	Undocumented, Risk is managed by individual capabilities
Preliminary	Partially Documented, Risk is managed by individual departments
Defined	Policies and procedures have been set by the organization, these are untested, and risk is evaluated and determined by executive leadership
Integrated	Policies and procedures have been set by the organization, these are tested and measured for effectiveness. Priority is managing list of risks, executives separate company goals and performance from risk.
Optimized	Policies and procedures have been set by the organization, these are tested and are embedded into strategic planning, focus is taking steps towards success not just attempting to avoid failures. Risk management is baked-in from the beginning. KPI and KRI are utilized to ensure progress towards business objectives.

Risk frameworks

**Operationally Critical Threat, Asset, and
Vulnerability Evaluation (OCTAVE):** a framework
that is used to understand what assets in an
organization are at risk. Utilizes three
phases.

Phase 1: build threat profiles for assets
Phase 2: identify vulnerabilities
Phase 3: develop a plan\

Information Technology Infrastructure Library (ITIL): a collection of precise methods for optimizing information technology asset management by increasing efficiency, decreasing risk, and boosting security

1. improving IT efficiency
2. reducing IT related risk
3. enhancing IT security

Threat Agent Risk Assessment (TARA): a practical methodology utilized to identify, assess, prioritize, and control risk.

Factor Analysis of Information Risk (FAIR): a framework aimed at giving the leadership of organization an accurate threat picture.

Committee of Sponsoring Organizations (COSO): the integrated framework provides a breakdown of into eight components: internal environment, objective setting, event identification, risk assessment, risk response, control activities, information and communication, and monitoring.

1.11 Understand and apply threat modeling concepts and methodologies

STRIDE threat modeling:

- Spoofing—a user or program pretends to be another
- Tampering—attackers modify components or code
- Repudiation—threat events are not logged or monitored
- Information disclosure—data is leaked or expose
- Denial of service (DoS)—services or components are overloaded with traffic to prevent legitimate use
- Escalation of privileges—attackers grant themselves additional privileges to gain greater control over a system

Process for Attack Simulation and Threat Analysis (PASTA:

1. Define business objectives
2. Define the technical scope of assets and components
3. Application decomposition and identify application controls
4. Threat analysis based on threat intelligence
5. Vulnerability detection
6. Attack enumeration and modeling
7. Risk analysis and development of countermeasures

Common Vulnerability Scoring System (CVSS)

CVSS provides a way to capture the principal characteristics of a vulnerability and produce a numerical score reflecting its severity. The numerical score can then be translated into a qualitative representation (such as low, medium, high, and critical) to help organizations properly assess and prioritize their vulnerability management processes.

MITRE Adversarial Tactics, Techniques, and Common Knowledge (ATT&CK)

The ATT&CK knowledge base is used as a foundation for the development of specific threat models and methodologies in the private sector, in government, and in the cybersecurity product and service community.

1.12 Apply Supply Chain Risk Management (SCRM) concepts

The Cybersecurity and Infrastructure Security Agency (CISA) a component under the Department for Homeland Security (DHS) has published 6 essential steps to building an effective SCRM practice:

1. Identify the people involved
2. Manage security, develop security policies

3. Assess the components
4. Know the supply chain and suppliers
5. Verify third parties, assess security
6. Evaluate systems for checking and auditing

Risks associated with hardware

Hardware is a great place for an exploit as they can be easily hidden and difficult to detect and made to look like legitimate components and survive software resets.

It is important to know where your vendors source parts, what factories are assembling the components and what security controls manufactures have for their employees and systems.

Risk associated with software

Software is a good choice for exploits as it does not require extra hardware to be inserted and is much cheaper to implement, although if detected can be removed more easily and is also easier to detect.

It is important to know where your vendors source their firmware and what controls are in place to ensure that the software that

is installed on your devices does not contain
any driver level or kernel level implants.

Risk associated with services

Services that your company utilizes need
to be trusted and reputable to ensure that any
data provided to any service maintains the same
level of security your own company provides.
Contractual agreements should be used to ensure
minimum security standards and accountability
for failure to meet the standards.

Minimum security requirements

Baseline of security requirements to
ensure that critical business assets are not at
risk. This is a standard that should be
implemented throughout an enterprise and should
consider all stakeholders in the enterprise
security team.

Third-party assessment and monitoring

It may be necessary to have a third party
inspect and monitor the supply chain to ensure
that contractual standards are being met, this
can ensure quality and can transfer risk to
another entity if there is an issue in the
supply chain.

Service level requirements

Service Level Requirement (SLR): requirements
for a service from the customers point of view

Service Level Agreement (SLA): agreement
between IT service provider and customer to
guarantee a service or performance level.
Penalties for failure are spelled out in the
contract

Service Level Report: insight into a service provider ability to deliver the agreed upon service quality.

1.13 Establish and maintain a security awareness, education, and training program

---

Methods and techniques to present awareness and training

User Security Awareness: security knowledge that leads to proper security behavior, awareness is having knowledge of a situation or fact

User Security Training: a structured approach for educating staff about computer security, training teaches tools, skills and competencies

Periodic content reviews

As part of due diligence, periodic content reviews should include updating training to reflect any recent legal changes, security tools, policy updates and specific attack vectors seen by the company.

User Access: user access should be reviewed periodically to ensure that user don't have permissions to data they are not entitled to.

Program effectiveness evaluation

Auditing: perform spot checks to ensure compliance with rules and standards

Testing: performing mock tests, such as phishing campaign to see if employees utilize security training

Penetration Testing: Regarding user training, penetration testing could include social engineering tactics such as including attachments from an untrusted source, piggybacking and tailgating.

Piggybacking: The act of following someone through a protected gate or gateway without being personally verified or permitted, with the consent of the person you are following.

Tailgating: The act of following someone into a secured area without the consent or knowledge of the person they are following.

Terms and Definitions:

Asset Value (AV): The monetary value of any given asset

Exposure Factor (EF): Percentage of loss to a specific asset

Single Loss Expectancy (SLE): Monetary cost of a single successful attack or threat realization **(SLE = AV * EF)**

Annual Rate of Occurrence (ARO): The number of losses that are expected to happen in an average year(s)

Annual Loss Expectancy (ALE): Annual monetary cost that is expected **(ARO * SLE)**

Business Impact Analysis (BIA):
Business Continuity Plan (BCP):
Disaster Recovery Plan (DRP):
Business Continuity Plan (BCP):

Recovery Time Objective (RTO): Time needed to get the critical functions running again

Maximum Tolerable Downtime (MTD): Maximum amount of time a business can tolerate an

outage before it cripples the business MTD =
RTO + WRT

Maximum Allowed Downtime (MAD): Maximum amount
of time a business can tolerate an outage
before it cripples the business MTD = RTO + WRT

Mean Time to Restore (MTTR): The average time
it takes to restore/repair

Work Recovery Time (WRT): Time needed to
configure and verify the integrity of a
recovered system

Mean Time Between Failure (MTBF): A measure of
how reliable hardware product or component is

Recovery Point Objective (RPO): Goal for how
recent your latest backup/snapshot was. Point
to "roll-back" to

Category	MTD
Tier 1	Minutes to an hour
Tier 2	24 hours
Tier 3	72 hours
Tier 4	7 Days
Tier 5	30 Days

Domain 2: Asset Security (10%)

2.1 Identify and classify information and assets

Classification

A process in which you determine the value of an asset and affix it a label, marking, or tag such as confidential, secret, or top secret. The label that an asset is assigned assists with determining the security precautions necessary to protect each of your assets.

Data classification

A process in which security labels are affixed to data based on the value of the data and restricts data to be seen by those with appropriate clearances.

Asset Classification

A process in which assets are given a label based on the value, and possibly the data they contain. Assets with certain labels may have higher protection levels, for example an information system with Top Secret data will only be located in a secure facility.

2.2 Establish information and asset handling requirements

Information Technology Infrastructure Library (ITIL): a collection of precise methods for optimizing information technology asset management by increasing efficiency, decreasing risk, and boosting security

2.3 Provision resources securely

Information and asset ownership

Information Ownership: legal rights and full control over a single data element or combination of data pieces

Asset Ownership: material and immaterial assets possessed by your company and/or required to run your company

Asset inventory

Organizations should have tools to manage asset inventory to be able to locate, identify and classify their assets, these tools should keep track of the assets value, name, owner and location at a minimum. It may be recommended to utilize separate tools to keep track of tangible vs intangible assets.

Tangible Assets: physical assets, like property, inventory, hardware

Intangible Assets: assets that do not physically exist, this can be patents, trade secrets, databases, software

Center for Internet Security (CIS): CIS Control 1 — Inventory and Control of Enterprise Assets and CIS Control 2 — Inventory and Control of Software Assets provide industry best practices for asset inventory.

Asset management

Configuration Management: A management process designed to keep computer systems, servers, and software at a consistent state throughout an enterprise.

Baselining: the bare minimum of security controls required to protect the information systems of an enterprise

2.4 Manage data lifecycle

Data roles

Data Subject: any individual natural person who can be identified, directly or indirectly, via an identifier

Data Owner: the entity that hold the legal right and control over a set of data

Data Steward: a role that is responsible for ensuring the quality and fitness of the organizations data assets

Data Custodian: a role that is responsible for the safe custody, transport, and storage of data and implementation of organizations rules

Data Processor: a natural or legal person, public authority, agency which processes data on behalf of the controller

Data collection

At the moment you collect personal data from a user you must inform them of the use of the data. It is good practice to only collect data that is necessary, as the data needs to be maintained and stored.

Data location

Where data is stored must also be outlined in policy. If data will be stored on

site or in the cloud, and if the data will be
stored online or offline.

Data maintenance

Data should be updated if any changes,
new releases, or alterations to the original
data have taken place.

Data retention

Data retention is based on preserving and
maintaining useful information for as long as
it is required, and then destroying it in a
secure manner when its existence is no longer
required, this should be set forth by corporate
data retention policies.

Data remanence

Data that survives after noninvasive
measures of erasure have been exhausted. The
most common methods that leave data remanence
are deleting, formatting and overwriting.

Data destruction

There are two general types of data
destruction, soft destruction consists of
overwriting, deleting, and formatting. The
second is full physical destruction, this uses
disk crushers, shredders and incinerators, it
is good practice to soft destroy data prior to
full physical destruction, this way data cannot
be stolen while the disk is in transit to be
destroyed.

Overwriting: a process to reuse the physical
disk by overwriting all the data on the disk,
this is not secure as data can still typically
be recovered in a lab, and should only be used
for use in the same classification as original
data

Purging: a process in which data is removed from the disk in a way that data will not be able to be recovered, disk is not intended for reuse

Degaussing: a process that destroys magnetic media only, this is done by exposing the media to a strong magnetic field, disk is not intended for reuse, does not work on Solid State Drives

Destruction: a process that the physical disk is destroyed and is no longer readable rendering it incapable of storing data, this is done by disk crushers, shredders, incinerating, pulverizing and acid.

Crypto Shredding: a process in which the data is stored encrypted on a disk and the encryption key is permanently destroyed or deleted, this can be useful in cloud, or third party hosted environments

2.5 Ensure appropriate asset retention

End of Life

A product that a vendor no longer markets or sells, does not plan to sustain due to product reaching the end of its useful life.

End of Support

A product that a vendor no longer supports, this can be through warranty or software update, typically vendor will offer alternative options, and will not replace or support that exact product.

2.6 Determine data security controls and compliance requirements

Data states

Data at rest: data stored in any form

Data in motion: data currently traveling

Data in use: data currently in RAM or being processed

Scoping and tailoring

Scoping: eliminating non-applicable baseline security requirements, such as privacy controls where private data does not exist

Tailoring: changing the baseline to make it more appropriate to your specific use case

Supplement: adding to the baseline

Standards selection

The process in which it is determined which framework to utilize to create a baseline for an organization. As there are many different standards it is recommended to use multiple different frameworks and security standards to ensure that there are minimal gaps in your security program.

Data protection methods

Digital Rights Management (DRM): uses encryption to enforce copyright restriction on digital media. This is done to protect intellectual property

Data Loss Prevention (DLP): detects potential data breaches/data ex-filtration transmissions and prevents them by monitoring, detecting, and blocking sensitive data while in use, in motion, and at rest.

Cloud Access Security Broker (CASB): A cloud access security broker is on-premises or cloud-based software that sits between cloud service users and cloud applications and monitors all activity and enforces security policies.

Link Encryption: a method in which a network communication is encrypted and decrypted at each level, or node. It is used to prevent traffic analysis and hide origin headers.

End to End Encryption (E2EE): a secure communication method that prohibits third parties from accessing data while it is being transported from one end system to another

Domain 3: Security Architecture and Engineering (13%)

3.1 Research, implement and manage engineering processes using secure design principles

---

Threat modeling

Threat models create a standardized structured approach to identifying threats and categorizing them based on the risk to the network. Threat modelling is attack centric and requires that you identify assets that you are protecting and the potential vulnerabilities those assets have

STRIDE and DREAD threat modeling:

STRIDE is used to identify and classify the threats and DREAD is used to prioritize severity of the threat. DREAD Risk = (Damage + Reproducibility + Exploitability + Affected Users + Discoverability) / 5. This will result in a number between 1 and 10, with the higher number meaning more risk.

STRIDE:

- **S**poofing—a user or program pretends to be another
- **T**ampering—attackers modify components or code
- **R**epudiation—threat events are not logged or monitored
- **I**nformation disclosure—data is leaked or expose
- **D**enial of service (DoS)—services or components are overloaded with traffic to prevent legitimate use
- **E**scalation of privileges—attackers grant themselves additional privileges to gain greater control over a system

DREAD:

- **D**amage Potential – how much damage will be caused?
  - o (0=nothing,5=info disclosure, 8=user data, 10=destruction)
- **R**eproducibility – how easy is it to reproduce the exploit?
  - o (0=very hard, 5=hard, 7.5=authenticated user,10=easy)
- **E**xploitability – what is needed to exploit the threat?
  - o (0=advanced,5=public,9=proxy,10=any browser)
- **A**ffected users – how many users will be affected?
  - o (0=none,2.5=individual,6=some individual,8=admins, 10=all)
- **D**iscoverability – how easy is it to discover the vulnerability?
  - o (0=very hard,5=http manipulation,8=public, 10=visible)

Process for Attack Simulation and Threat Analysis (PASTA:

8. Define business objectives
9. Define the technical scope of assets and components
10. Application decomposition and identify application controls
11. Threat analysis based on threat intelligence
12. Vulnerability detection
13. Attack enumeration and modeling
14. Risk analysis and development of countermeasures

Common Vulnerability Scoring System (CVSS)

CVSS provides a way to capture the principal characteristics of a vulnerability and produce a numerical score reflecting its severity. The numerical score can then be translated into a qualitative representation (such as low, medium, high, and critical) to help organizations properly assess and prioritize their vulnerability management processes.

MITRE Adversarial Tactics, Techniques, and Common Knowledge (ATT&CK)

The ATT&CK knowledge base is used as a foundation for the development of specific threat models and methodologies in the private sector, in government, and in the cybersecurity product and service community.

Least privilege

Least Privilege: the concept that users/system are only given access to what they need to complete their job, no more or less, exactly what they need

Defense in depth

Defense in Depth: layered defensive controls

Secure defaults

secure defaults principle says that the systems we design should default to a secure mode if we don't do anything else.

Fail securely

When a component, program, or device is in an inconsistent state, it is configured to fail in a controlled manner that precludes exploitation.

Physical Security: doors fail locked
Logical Security: fail with data secure

Separation of Duties (SoD)

The concept of separation of duties is used to prevent fraud and error, this is accomplishing by requiring more than one person to complete a task. This can be seen in the Clark Wilson model and the Chinese Wall model.

Keep it simple

A design principle that computer systems should be kept to simple solutions and avoid unnecessary complications

Zero Trust

A strategic initiative that helps prevent successful data breaches by eliminating the concept of trust from an organization's network architecture.

Privacy by design

A framework based on proactively embedding privacy into the design and operation of IT systems, networked infrastructure, and business practices.

Trust but verify

A security approach that you would initially trust devices but verify that they meet security requirements after allowing them on the network

Shared responsibility

A cloud security framework that dictates the security obligations of a cloud computing provider and its users to ensure accountability.

3.2 Understand the fundamental concepts of security models

There are two types of security models **Confidentiality** models and **Integrity** models. Confidentiality models focused on aligning object labels with subject labels to ensure that subjects do not access object labels they do not have the permissions to view.

Bell-LaPadula (Confidentiality)

The Bell-LaPadula model is a lattice-based model that utilizes the access rights of subjects and the classification level of objects to determine if the subject has authorization to access the object.

Simple Security Property: states that subjects cannot access/read objects with higher level classification than their access rights

Star Security Property: states that subject cannot access/write to objects with a lower-level classification than their access rights

Discretionary Security Property: the access matrix or protection matrix has satisfied the requirements of both the Star Security Property and the Simple Security Property.

Strong Star Property: an alternative to the Star Security Property in which the subjects can only write/read at the same classification level.

Memory Trick: "write up, read down" (WURD) End phrase, "Read Down" has 8 letters and LaPadula has 8 letters

Chinese Wall (Confidentiality)

The purpose of the Chinese Wall model is to **prevent conflicts of interest**. This model is popular in finance where the advisory section is separated from the brokerage section, this separates those giving inside advice from those buying/selling stocks, to prevent insider trading. This model provides both privacy and integrity.

Biba (Integrity)

The purpose of the Biba Model is not to restrict access, but rather ensure the integrity of the data. The model is designed to protect against corrupted data and ensure that data of a lower integrity level does not corrupt data of a higher integrity level.

Simple Integrity Property: a subject may not read data from a lower integrity level.

Star Integrity Property: a subject may not write to a higher level of integrity.

Invocation Property: a subject cannot send messages to another subject with higher integrity

Memory Trick: "read up, write down" (RUWD) first word has 4 letters just like Biba

Clark Wilson (Integrity)

The purpose of the Clark Wilson model is to maintain information integrity, this model is particularly focused on preventing fraud. This is accomplished by granting access to objects via transformation procedures and a restricted interface.

Well Formed Transactions: transitions the system from one consistent state to another, keeping a log of the transaction.

Separation of Duties: requires that person requesting transaction is separate than person performing transaction.

Constrained Data Item (CDI): Data inside control zone, cannot be accessed directly by subject

Integrity Verification Procedure (IVP): performs authentication and authorization, if successful subject given access to CDI

Transformation Procedure (TP): subject requests to access the CDI, converted into permissions and forwarded to IVP

Unconstrained Data Item (UDI): Data outside control zone, can be accessed directly by subject

3.3 Select controls based upon systems security requirements

Trusted Computer System Evaluation Criteria (TCESC): A US DoD evaluation standard for assessing the effectiveness of computer security controls

Level Label	Requirements
D	Minimal Protection
C1	Discretionary Protection
C2	Controlled Access Protection
B1	Labeled Security
B2	Structured Protection
B3	Security Domains
A1	Verified Protection

Information Technology Security Evaluation Criteria (ITSEC): A European derivative of TCSEC, that would test for functionality and assurance levels, has been mostly replaced by Common Criteria.

Common Criteria: Newest international system to evaluate security functions, tests for functionality and assurance from independent labs.

Target of Evaluation: the product configuration, version, scope of security functionality being evaluated

Protection Profile: a requirements statement, published for specific types of technologies, specifies functional and assurance requirements

Security Target: A document written by the vendor of a product intended to describe how a product achieves the described requirements, includes the vendor desired EAL and protection profile to test the product against

Evaluation Assurance Level (EAL): a grade from EAL1 to EAL7 indicating the level of assurance that a product has been tested against, in increasing assurance levels additional requirements are added

EAL1: Functionally Tested
EAL2: Structurally Tested
EAL3: Methodically Tested and Checked
EAL4: Methodically Designed, Tested and Reviewed
EAL5: Semi formally Designed and Tested
EAL6: Semi formally Verified, Design and Tested
EAL7: Formally Verified Designed and Tested

3.4 Understand security capabilities of Information Systems (IS)

Trusted Computing Base (TCB)

Comprises all the security mechanisms, used to protect an information system, this includes all hardware, firmware and software that contribute to the overall security. All the protections discussed in this section are included in the TCB.

Reference Monitor: an abstract model or concept that enforce access controls and determine if subjects are able to access/modify objects through a process called mediation. The rules of this model say that the validation mechanism must be always invoked, verifiable, tamper proof and unable to be bypassed.

*Memory trick: Non-bypass, Evaluable, Always Invoked, Tamper Proof (NEAT)

*Note: TCSEC B3 and above must implement the reference monitor concept

Subject: a person or user

Security Kernel: an implementation of the reference monitor concept that operates on the concepts of completeness, isolation, and verifiability.

Central Processing Unit (CPU)

Control Unit: performs instructions that have been taken from memory

Arithmetic Logic Unit (ALU): performs mathematical and logical operations

Multi-threading: a program that has the capability to carry out more than one thread at a time

Multi-processing: two or more processor cores working on a different parts of a single application

Multi-tasking: capable of performing more than one task or subtasks at a given time

Multi-core: a processor that exists on a single circuit that contains multiple processing cores, each core is capable to read and execute instructions independent of the other

Data Hiding: running processes in lower privilege effectively hides processes that are in higher privileges

Processor States

Problem State: the standard or default condition in which user programs are executed, see also User Mode, Program State

Supervisor State: a specific mode of operation in which the user has no access, and the processor is solely controlled by the operating system, see also Kernel Mode, Privileged Mode

Process Isolation: processes do not have access to one another this can be accomplished with memory segmentation

Memory Segmentation: processes are given a block in memory that they are allowed to access, process cannot access blocks in memory that they are not assigned

Ring Protection Model:

The Ring protection concept is intended to be implemented by the processor and taken advantage of by the Operating System (OS), the idea is the innermost ring is the most protected, the kernel, and the further out you go the less protection there is

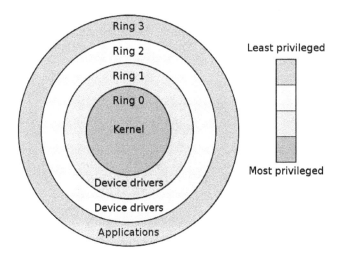

Memory Protection

Physical Memory: referring to the actual physical memory, typically Random-Access Memory

(RAM), but the cache and register are also physical memory.

Virtual Memory: refers to logical memory, which is a memory management technique that utilizes the hard disk to offload from physical memory. This allows for programmers and the operating system to use more memory for programs than physical memory is present on the system.

Random Access Memory (RAM): a volatile form of memory that can be directly accessed and content changed, two main types are Static RAM (SRAM) and dynamic RAM (DRAM). Static RAM uses semiconductors while DRAM uses capacitors.

Read Only Memory (ROM): non-volatile memory used in computers and other electrical devices Data contained in ROM cannot be rewritten.

Cache: memory that temporarily stores frequently executed instructions, utilized for quicker data processing

Register: the smallest and fastest memory in a computer, holding CPU instructions, perform mathematical operations, directly accessed by the CPU

Primary Storage: contains data that is currently in use, this includes RAM, cache and register

Secondary Storage: contains data that uses I/O bus to be accessed, this is the hard drive, external drives and removeable media.

Paging: is a memory management technique in which process address space is broken into blocks of the same size called **pages** (size is power of 2, between 512 bytes and 8192 bytes). The size of the process is measured in the number of pages.

Segmentation: memory management works very similar to paging but here segments are of variable-length whereas in paging pages are of fixed size.

Segmentation Fault: an error that occurs when an application attempts to access a block of memory that was not assigned to the application

Trusted Platform Module (TPM)

Trusted Platform Module (TPM): an international standard for a safe crypto processor, which is a dedicated microcontroller designed to secure hardware using integrated cryptographic keys.

Disk Encryption

Self-encrypting drive (SED): a hard disk drive (HDD) or solid-state drive (SSD) that has an encryption circuit. The disk does all of the encryption and decryption, not the computer's memory or processor. It transparently encrypts all data written to the media and transparently decrypts all data read from the media when unlocked.

Full Disk Encryption (FDE): encrypts the full disk and all its contents on an operating system level, this encrypts and decrypts when the OS is turned on/off. The OS typically uses the TPM to encrypt the drive. Bitlocker is used for Windows and FileVault is used for MacOS.

File Level Encryption (FLE): encrypts at the files system level, enabling encryption of specific files or directories.

Software

Operating System: software that supports the basic functions of a computing device, provides the input and output functions that interact with the user, execute programs and controls peripheral devices. Typically, can run user mode and kernel mode, separating the user from the core functionality of the operating system.

System Kernel: the lowest level of the operating system, the system kernel is in direct control of the hardware of a device and is executed from memory.

Firmware: a type of software that is embedded into the hardware, does not require an operating system, firmware provides the instructions for the device to function

Virtual Machine: a computer operating system that is installed via software instead of physically, this allows for one or more operating systems to be installed within a single physical set of hardware.

3.5 Assess and mitigate the vulnerabilities of security architectures, designs, and solution elements

Client-based systems

Client-based flaws expose the user, their data, and their system to assault, compromise, and destruction.

Server-based systems

Server based systems expose ports to the public and have services that are exposed to the public. Flaws can expose multiple users data, company data, databases and internal documents.

Database systems

Databases are behind almost all web forms and are vulnerable to many different types of attacks such as SQL injection.

Cryptographic systems

Cryptographic systems are vulnerable to many different types of attacks based on: key lifecycle, public key length, symmetric key lengths, storage of public and private keys, randomness of generated keys and the strength of the algorithm used.

Industrial Control Systems (ICS)

Programmable Logic controller (PLC): hardware-based system for reading a single instrument and controlling actuators, motors

Distributed control system (DCS): coordinates and supervises an entire plant of many varying processes and equipment

Supervisory Control and Data Acquisition (SCADA): computer system to gather, analyze, and control real time data for a variety of Industrial control systems

Cloud-based systems (e.g., Software as a Service (SaaS), Infrastructure as a Service (IaaS), Platform as a Service (PaaS))

Software as a Service (SaaS): applications and data

Platform as a Service (PaaS): servers, OSs, application, data

Infrastructure as a Service (IaaS): servers and operating systems

ID as a Service (IDaaS): authentication by service provider

Cloud Access Security Broker (CASB): A cloud access security broker is on-premises or cloud-based software that sits between cloud service users and cloud applications and monitors all activity and enforces security policies.

Distributed systems

Systems whose components are distributed over multiple networked computers and communicate and coordinate their actions by transferring messages from one system to another.

Internet of Things (IoT)

Devices embedded with sensors, processing power, software, and other technologies that communicate and exchange data with other devices and systems over the Internet or other communication networks.

Microservices

Small, independent services that are coupled together, but operate in separate codebases, that are managed by a development team.

Containerization

Self-contained unit of software that contains all dependencies and code packages needed to run applications in a lightweight package.

Serverless

A cloud computing execution model in which the cloud provider assigns machine resources on a per-request basis

Embedded systems

A computer processor, computer memory, and input/output peripheral devices combination that performs a specific function within a larger mechanical or electronic system.

High-Performance Computing (HPC) systems

The process of pooling computing capacity in order to solve huge issues in science, engineering, or business with substantially higher performance than a conventional desktop computer or workstation.

Edge computing systems

A distributed computing paradigm that moves computation and data storage closer to data sources

Virtualized systems

In a type 1, the hypervisor is installed bare metal on the server, meaning the hypervisor is the base operating system. In a type 2, the hypervisor is a piece of software that runs on top of the operating system.

Type 1: Hypervisor Architecture

Type 2: Host Operating System Architecture

Virtual Machine (VM): a computer operating system that is installed via software instead of physically, this allows for one or more

operating systems to be installed within a
single physical set of hardware.

3.6 Select and determine cryptographic solutions

Cryptographic life cycle (e.g., keys, algorithm selection)

Data Encryption Standard (DES): developed in
the 1970s DES is a symmetric key algorithm with
a key length of 56 bits, considered insecure
due to its short key length it was publicly
broken in 1997

Triple DES (3DES): proposed in 1981 3DES is a
symmetric key block cipher, 3DES applies the
DES algorithm three times to each block of
data. Both DES and 3DES are considered
deprecated since 2017

Rivest Cipher 4 (RC4): designed in 1987, RC4 is
a symmetric stream algorithm with key sizes
between 40 and 2048 bits. Used in WEP, WPA and
SSL and TLS

Rivest Shamir Adleman (RSA): developed in 1977,
RSA is an asymmetric public key algorithm. Used
in PGP and GPG.

Advanced Encryption Standard (AES): first
published in 1998, AES is a symmetric algorithm
with key sizes 128,192 and 256 bits and block
size of 128 bits.

Twofish: published in 1998, 2fish is a
symmetric key block cipher with a block size of
128 and key sizes of 128, 192 and 256 bits.

Key life cycle:
- Generation of new keys
- Keys are Used
- Keys are Stored
- Keys are Archived
- Keys are Deleted

Cryptographic life cycle phases
1. Acceptable: safe to use, no known security risk
2. Deprecated: allowed, but has risk
3. Restricted: use is deprecated plus additional restrictions
4. Legacy use: algorithms only used to process data already encrypted

Cryptographic methods (e.g., symmetric, asymmetric, elliptic curves, quantum)

Symmetric: utilizes a single, secret key, for both encryption and decryption, function in two modes, stream or block mode, RC4, AES, DES, 3DES are examples of symmetric encryption

Number of Keys = N * (N-1) / 2

Block Modes:

Electronic code Block (ECB): typically used for encrypting small, independent blocks of information

Cipher Block Chaining (CBC): typically used for encrypting files, docs, storage, media, eliminates repeating patterns.
Stream Modes:

Cipher Feed Back (CFB): Typically used for encrypting streaming communications

Output Feed Back (OFB): also, for streaming. Provides pre-processing of the next key, faster than CFB

Counter Mode (CTR): Streaming but fastest speed advantage. Provides parallel preprocessing of all keys at once

CBC and CFB errors will propagate; each encrypted block affects the next encryption. ECB, OFB and CTR errors do not propagate.

One Time Pad: Invented by Gilbert Vernam who also invented the stream cipher
  4 rules of OTP:
    1. Key must contain all random characters
    2. Key must be at least if the message itself
    3. Key must be used only once
    4. Key must be securely disposed of after use

Block ciphers: work in two modes (block or stream mode)
    1. To encrypt data at rest (block)
    2. Or data in transit (stream)

Stream Cipher: to encrypt data in transit
Uses pseudo random number generator to create a keystream that way the key doesn't just repeat over and over

Asymmetric: utilizes a pair of keys, one public key and one private key, data is encrypted with public key and can only be decrypted with the private key. RSA, ECC, Diffie-Hellman,

        Number of Keys = N + N

Asymmetric methods
    1. Confidentiality or secure-message format, use receivers public key
    2. Proof of origin, or open-message format. Use sender's private key to encrypt with first

3. Confidentiality and proof of origin or secure and signed message format\

Private key protection: as a rule, never give your private key to anyone, except to back up your private key

Mathematical methods used for asymmetric encryption include:
1. Factoring the product of two large prime numbers
2. Discrete logarithms in a finite field
3. knapsack algorithm

Hybrid cryptography — combining symmetric systems and asymmetric key exchange

- RSA (key exchange)
- ElGamal (key exchange)
- Elliptic Curve Cryptography (ECC) (key exchange)
- Diffie-Helman (uses discrete logarithm) (key negotiation)
- Digital Signature Algorithm (DSA): only used for digital signatures

Elliptical curve cryptography (ECC): utilizes the algebraic structure of elliptic curves over finite fields to generate a public-key pair that allows for smaller key sizes, with equivalent security

Quantum: utilizes quantum theory to distribute symmetric encryption keys, this can be thought of more accurately as quantum key distribution (QKD)

Public Key Infrastructure (PKI)

Public Key Infrastructure (PKI) is essential in today's digital world in authenticating users and devices. The key principle behind PKI is trust, certificates are created by trusted third party Certificate Authorities and issued to verified entities, which are then served to the subjects accessing the verified entities resources.

Certificate: is a digital document that is used to prove ownership of a public key.

X.509: international standard for digital certificates, used in TLS/SSL

Certificate Authority (CA): issues certificates, delegates provisioning authority to RA, publishes the CRL, the root CA should be kept offline

Intermediate Authority (CA): issues certificates

Registration Authority (RA): allowed by the CA to provision certificates to users

Certificate Revocation List (CRL): a digital list of certificates that have been revoked that is maintained on the CA

Online Certificate Status Protocol (OCSP): a protocol used for obtaining the revocation status of X.509 certificate

Key management practices

NIST SP 800-57: Recommendation for Key Management

Key lifecycle: keys should be cryptographically strong, rotated regularly and when no longer used deleted

Key Recovery: can be accomplished with split knowledge, dual control, or key escrow

Key Escrow: an escrow agency is given keys that are needed to decrypt encrypted data, access to the keys is controlled by the escrow agency, the key owner and in some cases an authorized third party can access the keys.

Kerckhoff principal: the concept that a Cryptographic system should be designed to be secure, even if all its details, except for the key, are publicly known.

Key Distribution: the process or way secret key pairs are exchanged

Digital signatures and digital certificates

Digital Signatures: Provide integrity, authenticity, and non-repudiation (origin, delivery)

Digital Signature Algorithm (DSA): a Federal Information Processing Standard (FIPS) discrete logarithm algorithm used for digital signatures only.

x.509 Digital Certificates: Used to verify the owner of a public key, contains the CA name, CA signature, certificate serial number issued by CA, validity dates, CRL location, subject public key and X.500 name.

non-repudiation

Provides accounting so that neither the sender or receiver of data can claim they did not receive the data or that they data was modified.

Origin: sender cannot deny that they sent the message

Delivery: receiver cannot deny that they received the message

Integrity (e.g., hashing)

Hash functions are one-way algorithms that transform a given string of text or data and represent them as a digest, hash code, hash value or simply hash, typically a fixed length string representation of the original data.

Collisions: occurs when two or more unique inputs to a hashing algorithm provide the same hash value, message, digest

Hash Collision Attacks: an attack that attempts to find two inputs that produce the same hash result

Rainbow Tables: a linked list of precomputed hash values, typically used as a means to lookup a password hash value and get the corresponding plaintext value

3.7 Understand methods of cryptanalytic attacks

Brute force

Brute force: Attempts to determine a secret by trying *every possible combination*, number of attempts will only be limited by length of password and number of characters allowed.

Dictionary attack: slightly more efficient than brute forcing, this attack uses a precompiled list of most common passwords and words

Ciphertext only

A cryptanalysis attack model in which the attacker is considered to only have access to the ciphertext and derive plaintext or key from the ciphertext

Known plaintext

An attack model for cryptanalysis where the attacker has access to both the plaintext, ciphertext, used to derive plaintext or key

Frequency analysis

An attack against ciphertext that takes advantage of frequency of words used in language to derive the plaintext.

Chosen ciphertext

A cryptanalysis attack model in which the cryptanalyst gathers information by decrypting selected ciphertexts the attacker can derive the concealed secret key

Implementation attacks

Attack exploits the methodology of implementation; this focuses mostly on exploiting the underlying software used by the encryption system.

Side-channel

An attack that is primary focuses on taking advantage of the system running the encryption algorithm, instead of weaknesses of the algorithm

Fault injection

An attack that causes the system running the encryption system to fault and cause the system to change its normal behavior.

Timing

A specific type of side-channel attack that compromises the timing system used by a cryptosystem in an attempt to break the cryptosystem.

Man-in-the-Middle (MITM)

An attack that inserts a system between two systems that trust they are directly communicating with each other.

Pass the hash

An attack that exploits authentication mechanism, by providing the hash value instead of the user password, this is frequently used in lateral movement

Kerberos exploitation

Golden Ticket: the Kerberos authentication token for the KRBTGT account, a special hidden account tasked with encrypting all the DC's authentication tokens, the ticket can be used to log into any account using a pass-the-hash strategy, commonly referred to as pass-the-ticket.

Ransomware

An attack the encrypts data on a victim computer, and sells the key to the user, in the event the user does not pay, all the data is effectively crypto-shredded and lost.

Types of Attacks

Passive Attacks: the attacker is able to access assets on your network, the attacker is sniffing traffic and simply collecting, at this stage the attacker is not sending traffic or interacting with the network.

Active Attacks: the attacker has gained access to assets on your network by interacting with your network, exploiting weaknesses in the network, at this stage the attack is able to control or change environment variables on your assets

Pretext Attack: this is a social engineering attack in which the attacker convinces the victim to perform adverse actions on their own systems or allows attacker to access their systems

Baiting Attack: a form of social engineering in which the attacker leaves a malicious item for an employee to plug in to the network

3.8 Apply security principles to site and facility design

Defense in depth should be the focus of your site and facility design, each layer of security should be complemented by another layer of security. Security systems should have redundancies and backups in place in case of failures. The security of the facility should also be commensurate of what the facility is being used for, while it is possible to over secure an area.

Site and Building Security Considerations:

- Power Sources
  - Enough room for backup generators/solar/wind
  - Stable primary power
- Distance from roads
  - Fencing with steel cable to prevent vehicle incursion
  - Use of bollards at guard stations/drains/creeks
- Distance from walkways
  - Strain sensitive fencing to detect climbing or cutting
  - Regular security patrols along high traffic walkways
- Distance between fence line and buildings
  - Motion detectors to detect perimeter breach
  - PTZ cameras to monitor perimeter
- Perimeter and Property Lighting
  - Well lit properties tend to discourage criminal activity
  - Cameras can detect motion better in lit areas
  - IR LED for night vision in cameras can be easily defeated

- Environmental concerns
  - Flood plain
  - Forest fires/hurricanes/tornadoes
- Camera Placement
  - Ensure that there are no blind spots
  - Best practice is to overlap camera sightlines
- Fencing
  - Perimeter fence height can determine if an intruder is successful
    - 3-4 ft will deter casual trespassers
    - 6-7 ft is not easy to climb/block vision
    - 8 ft delays even determined intruders
  - Fencing construction such as solid metal, chain link
  - No holes along the ground with creeks and drains
- Mantraps and turnstiles
- Security Glass
  - Plate glass – standard glass, lowest cost
  - Tempered glass – used in windshield anti shatter
  - Wired glass – glass will shatter but not allow you through
  - Laminated glass – two plates of glass with plastic layer in middle
  - Acrylic glass – highly resilient but toxic in fire
  - Polycarbonate – highly resistant, flame inhibiting, higher cost
- Badged access for buildings
- Badged access for office spaces
- Emanations
  - Tempest specifications
  - Laser mics to windows
  - Data center/servers in the middle of facility
- Security Cameras
  - PTZ – Pan, Tilt and Zoom
  - Focal Length – lower the number = wider view
  - F-stop – lower the number = less depth of field

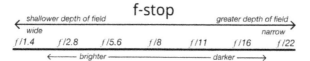

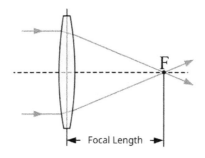

Focal Length

3.9 Design site and facility security controls

Wiring closets/intermediate distribution facilities

When considering site security regarding cabling it is important to consider access to cables, switches, firewalls, and routers. The MDF and IDF should be secured in manner that you can control who has access and also have a record of access, it is additionally important to ensure that the cables ingress and egress point are secure and that cables are not exposed.

Main Distribution Frame (MDF): typically, the demarcation point that houses the edge router and firewall

Intermediate Distribution Facility (IDF): connected to the MDF and typically houses switches, internal routers, and internal firewalls, this can be a distribution point located on a floor or building

Patch Panel: a cable connection point that allows for flexibility in arranging the termination point of cables.

Server rooms/data centers

Server rooms and data centers should have a high level of security and should at a minimum have an access control mechanism that records ingress and egress as well as CCTV cameras inside and at the entry point. It is ideal to have access limited to a single point. All servers should be in locked racks have the ability to record who has accessed a specific rack.

There are also additional considerations that should be made such as sensors for temperature, humidity, smoke, water to ensure that the servers are not damaged from environmental hazards.

Media storage facilities

Media storage should be in a site that is geographically separated from your server rooms and datacenters, this would ensure that if your servers suffer from a disaster the media needed to recover would not be affected by the same disaster. The facilities should have the same care taken as your data center security and should also have the same environmental sensors to ensure that the media is not damaged while in storage.

Media that is placed into storage should be checked into the facility and a hash of the storage medium should be accomplished to ensure that if the medium is checked out the integrity of the data can be verified.

Evidence storage

Evidence storage has additional security requirements that need to be considered such as a mechanism to check-in a piece of evidence, to record every time evidence is accessed and a way to check out evidence. These steps are required to ensure the chain of custody. Policies should be enacted that detail who is allowed to access the evidence room and should also require two-person integrity to access evidence.

The evidence room should have CCTV cameras both inside the room and at the entry and exit. A log should be kept of time and date of anyone that enters the evidence rooms. Security sensors and environmental sensors should be installed to ensure that the evidence is not compromised by break in or by environmental hazards.

Restricted and work area security

Restricted areas are often utilized to ensure a high level of security for sensitive data, such as a Secure Compartmented Information Facility (SCIF). A SCIF and restricted access facilities can ensure that only authorized personnel are able to access the facility and the resources available to the facility.

It is important that users are trained in workplace security, this mean not keeping papers out on the desk and ensuring that screens are placed at an angle that does not allow shoulder surfing.

Utilities and Heating, Ventilation, and Air Conditioning (HVAC)

HVAC systems are critical for the safe and continued use of computing and networking equipment as these systems are easily damaged from excessive heat, and low and high humidity.

Due care should be taken to ensure that the heat load of the servers can be handled by the HVAC units and that the server room is well insulated and ventilated. Some key

considerations to make for your server room
are:

- Ideal temperature: 59 °F to 89.6 °F / 15 °C to 32 °C
- Ideal Humidity: 40% to 60% Relative Humidity (rH)
- Hot and Cold aisles should be established
- Racks should remain locked and closed with blanking panels for empty slots to ensure integrity of hot/cold aisles

Environmental issues

There are always environmental concerns when looking at site selection, such as flood plains, hurricanes, tornadoes, and earthquakes. All factors should be considered when selecting a site and an appropriate plan should be put into place to mitigate risk.

Flooding is an especially large risk with server rooms as there is electrical cables that are typically ran under the floor which could lead to destruction of servers and data. It is incredibly important that water sensors be placed in strategic areas that will alert of the presence of water before it could cause damage.

Fire prevention, detection, and suppression

Protecting personnel should always be the first goal of any fire prevention plan, the protection of equipment and servers should always be secondary to protecting human life.

There are three main detection systems: ionization, photoelectric and combination.

There are four main suppression systems: wet pipe, dry pipe, deluge and preaction.

There are five types fire extinguishers: Class A, B, C, D and K. Fire extinguishers should be 50' from equipment and near doors

Ionization: best at detecting fast flaming fires, this sensor works by detecting smoke that enters the ionized air between two plates.

Photoelectric: best at detecting slow smoldering fires, this sensor works by reflecting light into a light sensor when smoke enters the chamber.

Combination: a combination of ionization and photoelectric sensors best at detecting both fast and slow burning fires, however combination sensors don't perform either function as well as the dedicated sensor.

Wet Pipe: this suppression system is always full of water, once a sprinkler head is activated the water will release from that sprinkler head.

Dry Pipe: this suppression system is full of pressurized air, once a sprinkler head is activated the air is released which allows the water to fill the pipes and release from the triggered sprinkler head.

Deluge: this suppression system is full of unpressurized air and all sprinkler heads are open, when triggered water is flooded into the pipes are released from all sprinkler heads.

Preaction: this suppression system is full of air, the water is released into the pipe if an alarm is triggered, but water is not released until a sprinkler head is triggered, at which point water is released from the triggered sprinkler head.

Class A: used for common combustibles that leave ash, uses water or soda acid for suppression, think of Class A for Ash

Class B: used for liquids that boil, uses CO_2, halon or soda acid for suppression, think of Class B for Boil

Class C: used for electrical fires, uses CO_2 or halon for suppression, think of Class C for electrical current

Class D: used for combustible metals, uses dry powder for suppression, think of Class D for Dynamite

Class K: used for kitchen fires, uses CO2 or halon for suppression, think of Class K for Kitchen

Class	Symbol	Type	Suppression Material
A		Common Combustibles (Ash)	Water, Soda Acid
B		Liquids(Boil)	CO2, Halon, Soda Acid
C		Electrical (Current)	CO2, Halon
D		Combustible Metal (Dynamite)	Dry Powder
K		Grease (Kitchen)	CO2, Halon

Power (e.g., redundant, backup)

Primary and Backup power are vitally important in the operation of a data center. It important that the primary power is stable and does not suffer from brownouts, blackouts, surges, swells. To ensure a stable primary supply an automatic voltage regulation (AVR) device should be utilized.

Backup power supply should be able to sustain the data center operations for short to long periods of power loss. This is typically accomplished by switching temporarily to a battery backup while a generator starts, once the generator is producing stable power the system switches from battery to the generator power.

Surge: also referred to as a spike, this is a short-term voltage increase and are typically caused by lightening, mis wired electrical, utility company load shifting.

Brownout: also referred to as a sag or undervoltage, this is a voltage deficiency. The most common causes are heavy load and poor circuit design.

Swell: this is an overvoltage condition, this is not the same as a surge which is a short-term or momentary increase, a swell is a voltage increase for a long duration. Common causes are sudden load reductions and oversupply by utility company.

Blackout: this is a complete loss of power. Common causes are tripped breakers, weather and accidents causing AC line disruption.

Redundant: a redundant power supply is a system which allows two identical power supplies to supply power to a single server, both power supplies are load balanced to ensure high availability power to the server, in the event one fails the other is able to sustain power to the server till the failed unit is replaced.

Electromagnetic interference (EMI): a phenomenon caused by electrical devices that create an electromagnetic field, electrical noise, that interferes with another electrical device. Can also occur naturally with sunspots, lightning, and auroras; most common with lights and running motors, also called **Radio Frequency Interference (RFI)** when it interferes with radio signals.

Domain 4: Communication and Network Security (13%)

4.1 Assess and implement secure design principles in network architectures

Open System Interconnection (OSI) and Transmission Control Protocol/Internet Protocol (TCP/IP) models

The OSI and TCP/IP models are conceptual models to describe the communication functions of computer systems, while the models are conceptual in nature they can help us mentally compartmentalize computer networks into layers or sections.

OSI Model:

7: Application: Interfaces with applications
6: Presentation: Protocols that ensure compatible syntax
5: Session: Protocols that coordinate exchange of information
4: Transport: Protocols responsible for end-to-end communications
3: Network: Protocols responsible for router to router
2: Data Link: Protocols responsible for node to node
1: Physical: Protocols responsible for the encoding and transmission of data onto network

TCP/IP Model:

Application Layer
Transport Layer
Internet Layer
Network Access Layer

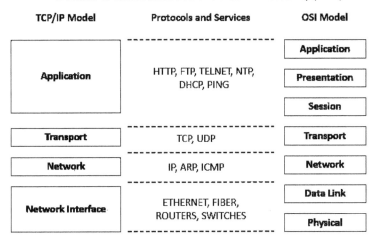

Data Encapsulation: taking the previous layer and encapsulating it as data and adding necessary data such as header information for the current layer

Data
TCP HEADER | DATA
IP HEADER | DATA
Ethernet HEADER | DATA

Internet Protocol (IP) networking (e.g., Internet Protocol Security (IPSec), Internet Protocol (IP) v4/6)

Internet Protocol Version 4 (IPv4): deployed in 1983, one of the core protocols used in networking, each address has 32 bits making a total of 4.2 billion IPv4 addresses. IPv4 is broken into different classes for internal networks.

Class Address Ranges	
Class A	1.0.0.0 - 126.0.0.0
Class B	128.0.0.0 - 191.255.0.0
Class C	192.0.1.0 - 223.255.255.0

Reserved Addresses
10.0.0.0 -> 10.255.255.255
172.16.0.0 -> 172.31.255.255
192.168.0.0 -> 192.168.255.255
27.0.0.0 is reserved for loopback and IPC on the local host
224.0.0.0 -> 239.255.255.255 is reserved for multicast addresses

Below is an IPv4 header, it contains the IP version, length of the packet, source and destination address of the packet, length of the packet and the protocol being used.

IPv4 Header							
	0		1		2		3
0	IP Version	Header Length	TOS		Total Length		
4		IP Identification		X D M			
8	TTL		Protocol		Checksum		
12	Source Address						
16	Destination Address						
20	Optional Options						

IPV4 Internet Control Message Protocol (ICMP):
an internet protocol that is commonly used
inside networks to troubleshoot connectivity
issues, ICMP messages will give a type and code
to relay the problem with communication

Type	Code	Description
0	0	Echo Reply
3	0	Net Unreachable
	1	Host Unreachable
	2	Protocol Unreachable
	3	Port Unreachable
	4	Fragmentation Needed
	5	Source Route Failed
	6	Destination Network Unknown
	7	Destination Host Unknown
	8	Source Host Isolated
	9	Net Administratively Prohibited
	10	Host Administratively Prohibited
	11	Dest Net Unreachable for TOS
	12	Dest Host Unreachable for TOS
	13	Communication Administratively Prohibited
	14	Host Precedence Violation
	15	Precedence cutoff in effect
4	0	Source Quench (Deprecated)
5	0	Redirect Datagram for the Network
	1	Redirect Datagram for the Host
	2	Redirect Datagram for the TOS and Network
	3	Redirect Datagram for the TOS and Host
8	0	Echo
9	0	Normal router advertisement
	16	Does not route common traffic
11	0	Time to Live exceeded in Transit
	1	Fragment Reassembly Time Exceeded
12	0	Pointer indicates the error
	1	Missing a Required Option
	2	Bad Length
13	0	Timestamp
14	0	Timestamp Reply
15	0	Information Request (Deprecated)
16	0	Information Reply (Deprecated)
17	0	Address Mask Request (Deprecated)
18	0	Address Mask Reply (Deprecated)
30	0	Traceroute (Deprecated)

Internet Protocol Version 6 (IPv6): deployed in 2012, one of the core protocols used in networking, each address has 128 bits making a total of 2^{128} or 340 trillion trillion trillion addresses. IPv6 handles fragmentation and the reassembly of packet.

Below is the header for IPv6 you can compare it looks quite different than the IPv4 header on previous pages.

	IPv6 Header			
	0	1	2	3
0	Version	Traffic Class	Flow Label	
4	Payload Length		Next Header	Hop Limit
8	Source IP Network			
12	Source IP Network			
16	Source IP Interface			
20	Source IP Interface			
24	Destination IP Network			
28	Destination IP Network			
32	Destination IP Interface			
36	Destination IP Interface			

IPv6 ICMP: IPv6 has its own version of ICMP with separate types and error codes

Type	Code	Description
0	0	Echo Reply
3	0	Net Unreachable
	1	Host Unreachable
	2	Protocol Unreachable
	3	Port Unreachable
	4	Fragmentation Needed
	5	Source Route Failed
	6	Destination Network Unknown
	7	Destination Host Unknown
	8	Source Host Isolated
	9	Net Administratively Prohibited
	10	Host Administratively Prohibited
	11	Dest Net Unreachable for TOS
	12	Dest Host Unreachable for TOS
	13	Communication Administratively Prohibited
	14	Host Precedence Violation
	15	Precedence cutoff in effect
4	0	Source Quench (Deprecated)
5	0	Redirect Datagram for the Network
	1	Redirect Datagram for the Host
	2	Redirect Datagram for the TOS and Network
	3	Redirect Datagram for the TOS and Host
8	0	Echo
9	0	Normal router advertisement
	16	Does not route common traffic
11	0	Time to Live exceeded in Transit
	1	Fragment Reassembly Time Exceeded
12	0	Pointer indicates the error
	1	Missing a Required Option
	2	Bad Length
13	0	Timestamp
14	0	Timestamp Reply
15	0	Information Request (Deprecated)
16	0	Information Reply (Deprecated)
17	0	Address Mask Request (Deprecated)
18	0	Address Mask Reply (Deprecated)
30	0	Traceroute (Deprecated)

Transmission control protocol (TCP):
connection-oriented protocol, reliable
protocol, utilizes a 3-way handshake for a
graceful opening and closing of the connection

TCP Header			
0	1	2	3
Source Port		Destination Port	
Sequence Number			
Acknowledgment Number			
Source Address			
HL R Flags		Window Size	
Optional Options			

User Datagram Protocol (UDP): connectionless
protocol, does not expect acknowledgments, not
reliable

UDP Header			
0	1	2	3
Source Port		Destination Port	
Length		Checksum	

Dynamic Host Configuration Protocol (DHCP): a
client/server protocol that negotiates IP
addresses for clients on the network, the DHCP
server will give clients an IP address, subnet
mask, gateway, and the DNS server address.

Domain Name Service (DNS): a hierarchical naming system for computer and other resources connected to the internet and on private networks. It associates IP address and other information to Fully Qualified Domain

DNS Header			
0	1	2	3
Query ID		QR | Opcode | AA | TC | RD | RA | Z | AD | CD | Rcode	
Query Count		Answer Count	
Total Authority Resource Records		Total Additional Resource Records	
DNS Data			
Legend			
QR - Query[0] or Response[1], Opcode - Query[0], Inverse Query[1], Status[2], Notify[4], Update[5], AA - Authoritative Answer, TC - Truncated Response, RD - Recursion Desired, RA - Recursion Available, Z - Zero,			

Common Ports:

Port	Service/Proto	Port	Service/Proto	Port	Service/Proto
7	echo	514	syslog	1863	MSN
20	ftp-data	515		2082-2083	cPanel
21	ftp	520		2967	Symantec AV
42	name	521		3128	HTTP Proxy
43	nickname	554		3260	iSCSI target
49	TACACS	546-547		3306	MySQL
53	DNS	560		3389	MS RDP
67	bootps	563		3689	iTunes
68	bootpc	587		3690	subversion
69	tftp	593	Microsoft DCOM	4333	mSQL
70	gopher	631	Internet Printing	4664	Google Desktop
79	finger	636	LDAP SSL	4899	radmin
80	HTTP	646		5000	UPnP
88	kerberos	691	MS Exchange	5001	iperf
102	MS Exchange	860	ISCI	5432	PostgreSQL
110	POP3	873	rsync	5500	VNC Server
113	ident	902	smware server	6000-6001	X11
119	NNTP	989-990	FTP SSL	6665-6669	IRC
123	NTP	993	IMAP4 SSL	6679,6697	IRC SSL
135	Microsoft RPC	995	POP3 SSL	8000	Internet Radio
137-139	NetBIOS	1025	Microsoft RPC	8080	HTTP Proxy
143	IMAP4	1026-1029	Microsoft Messenger	8086-8087	Kaspersky AV
161-162	SNMP	1080	Socks Proxy	8200	VMware Server
177	XDMCP	1080	MyDoom	9100	HP JetDirect
179	BGP	1194	OpenVPN	9800	WebDAV
201	Appletalk	1241	Nessus		
264	BGMP	1311	Dell Open Manage		
318	TSP	1433-1434	Microsoft SQL		
389	LDAP	1512	WINS		
443	HTTPS	1589	CISCO VQP		
445	Microsoft DS	1701			
464	Kerberos	1723			
465	SMTP SSL	1741			
512	rexec	1755			
513	rlogin	1812-1813	RADIUS		

Routing Protocols:

Exterior Gateway Protocol (EGP): a protocol used to exchange routing tables between different networks, used in exterior networks

Border Gateway Protocol (BGP): a protocol used to exchange routing tables between networks, used in exterior networks

Routing Information Protocol (RIP): an internal network protocol that uses hop count as a routing metric

Open Shortest Path First (OSPF): an internal network protocol that uses link-state to determine routing path

Enhanced Interior Gateway Routing Protocol (EIGRP): an interior network protocol that uses distance-vector to determine routing path, proprietary to CISCO

Secure protocols

SSL and TLS are very similar as they have a common root. SSL has version SSL1, SSL2, SSL3 and rather than continue with SSL 4 the next iteration was called TLS 1. SSL was renamed so that it would not appear as thought the Internet Engineering Task Force (IETF) was not blanketly approving Netscape proprietary SSL protocol.

SSL	
SSL 1.0	Never publicly released
SSL 2.0	Released Feb 1995, used same keys for message authentication and encryption, vulnerable to MITM, Deprecated 2011 by RFC 6176
SSL 3.0	Released in 1996, vulnerable to POODLE attack, Deprecated 2015 by RFC 7568
TLS (Removed backwards **compatibility** with SSL in 2011)	
TLS 1.0	Released 1999, Deprecated March 2020
TLS 1.1	Released 2006, added protection against CBC attacks, Deprecated March 2020
TLS 1.2	Released 2008, replaced MD5-SHA1 with SHA256, added AES support

TLS 1.3	Released 2018, encrypted handshakes after ServerHello, removed MD5 and SHA-224, seperated key agreement and authentication algorithms

Secure Socket Layer (SSL): a security protocol used to establish an encrypted connection between a client and a server.

Transport Layer Security (TLS): a security protocol that replaced SSL used to establish an encrypted connection between a client and a server.

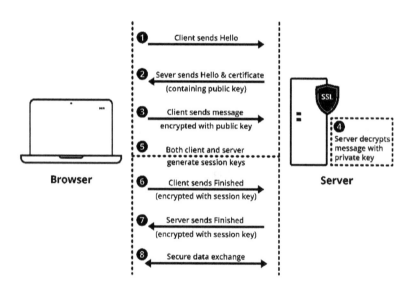

Implications of multilayer protocols

Multi-Layer protocols go across more than one layer of the OSI model, these allow for encryption to be integrated across layers and allows for greater flexibility, however this comes with risk as it makes it easier to create covert channels and bypass security controls that would be enforced at a specific layer.

Converged protocols (e.g., Fiber Channel Over Ethernet (FCoE), Internet Small Computer Systems Interface (iSCSI), Voice over Internet Protocol (VoIP))

The merger of specialty protocols with standard protocols can reduce costs as you do not require expensive proprietary hardware or software.

Fibre Channel over Ethernet (FCOE): a network encapsulation technique that sends Fibre Channel frames over 10 GbE.

Internet Small Computer Systems Interface (iSCSI): allows for SCSI commands to be sent over a TCP/IP network providing block level access to data storage facilities

Voice over Internet Protocol (VOIP): a technology that enable the use of voice calls over TCP/IP infrastructure, also called IP telephony.

Micro-segmentation (e.g., Software Defined Networks (SDN), Virtual eXtensible Local Area Network (VXLAN), Encapsulation, Software-Defined Wide Area Network (SD-WAN))

Microsegmentation: a method that allows the separation of logical zones in data centers and cloud environments that are individually isolated and secured for each micro segment

Software Defined Network (SDN): an approach to networking that enables different software to be installed on network hardware that can make the network more dynamic and efficient, the goal is to not be concerned with the underlying hardware and make the management and operation a simple process

Virtual eXtensible Local Area Network (VXLAN): a VLAN created in a virtual environment using software-defined (virtual) switches

Software-Defined Wide Area Network (SD-WAN): a virtual WAN architecture that allows enterprises to leverage any combination of transport services, including MPLS, LTE and broadband internet service, to securely connect users to applications

Wireless networks (e.g., Li-Fi, Wi-Fi, Zigbee, satellite)

IEEE Standard	Year Released	Speed	Frequency
802.11ax	2021	9.6 Gbps	2.4, 5 GHz
802.11ac	2012	1 Gbps	5 GHz
802.11n	2009	450 Mbps	2.4, 5 GHz
802.11g	2003	54 Mbps	2.4 GHz
802.11a	1999	54 Mbps	5 GHz
802.11b	1999	11 Mbps	2.4 GHz

Wired Equivalent Privacy (WEP): released in 1997 as the encryption mechanism for 802.11, utilizing RC4 and CRC-34 checksum, deprecated in 2004

WiFi Protected Access (WPA): released in 1999 as a replacement for WEP, WPA uses 64- or 128-bit keys, WPA replaced CRC with TKIP.

WiFi Protected Access 2 (WPA2): released in 2004 as a replacement for WPA, WPA2 supports CCMP which is based on AES encryption

WiFi Protected Access 3 (WPA3): released in 2018, uses 192 bit in enterprise mode and AES 256 in GCM mode and utilizes CCMP-128 as the minimum encryption, replaces pre-shared key with Simultaneous Exchange of Equals (SAE) for a more secure initial key exchange.

Service Set Identifier (SSID): the name that identifies a wireless network for the basic service set (BSS)

IEEE Standard	Year Released	Description
802.3	1973	Ethernet
802.11	1997	Wireless LAN
802.15	2002	Wireless PAN
802.15.1	2002	Bluetooth
802.15.4	2004	Low-Rate Wireless PAN (Zigbee)
802.1x	2001	Network Access Control

Bandwidth: maximum rate at which data can be transmitted
Latency: time delay between when data is sent and when it is received

Li-Fi: a wireless communication technology that utilizes light to transmit data and position between devices.

Zigbee: an IEEE 802.15.4-based specification used to create personal area networks with small, low-power, low-bandwidth devices, such as for home automation, medical device data collection, and small-scale projects that need a wireless connection.

Satellite: uses satellites in the atmosphere to transmit data.

Cellular networks (e.g., 4G, 5G)

Time Division Multiplexing (TDMA): a method by which multiple data signals are sent and received over a single signal path by utilizing synchronized switches and giving each data signal a "time slot"

Frequency Division Multiplexing (FDMA): a method by which multiple data signals are sent and received over a single signal path by dividing the total bandwidth into frequency bands, and each data signal is given its own frequency band

Time Division Multiple Access (TDMA): a method in which multiple users can share the same frequency channel by dividing the signal into time slots

Global System for Mobile Communications (GSM): a standard developed by the European Standards Institute for cellular communications, GSM used TDMA

Universal Mobile Telecommunication System (UMTS): a third generation mobile standard developed in 2001 based on the GSM standard

Code Division Multiple Access (CDMA): a method in which multiple users can share the same frequency channel by using coded transmitters that modulate the signal for each device, allowing for use of the full frequency spectrum

Generation	Signal Type	Year	Mutliplexing
1G	Analog	1979	FDMA
2G	Digital	1991	GSM
2G	Digital	1991	CDMA
3G	Digital	1998	UMTS
3G	Digital	1998	CDMA2000
4G	Digital	2009	LTE
5G	Digital	2016	5g NR

Content Distribution Networks (CDN)

Content Distribution Network (CDN):
geographically separated servers that cache
content and allow for end users to access
multimedia content from the nearest server to
their physical location, this allows for media
content to be accessed more quickly by the
client

4.2 Secure network components

Operation of hardware (e.g., redundant power, warranty, support)

Redundant: a redundant power supply is a system
which allows two identical power supplies to
supply power to a single server, both power
supplies are load balanced to ensure high
availability power to the server, in the event
one fails the other is able to sustain power to
the server till the failed unit is replaced.

Warranty: is the guarantee provided with a
purchased device that ensures replacement or
repair if the device fails within a certain
period of time.

Support: involves documenting the appropriate contact information so that the vendor or seller can be contacted during the warranty period for service.

Transmission media

Fast Ethernet: ethernet cables that can transfer data at a rate of 100 Mbps

Gigabit Ethernet: ethernet cables that can transfer data at a rate of 1 Gbps

10 Gigabit Ethernet: ethernet cables that can transfer data at a rate of 10 Gbps

Unshielded Twisted Pair (UTP): two conductors of a circuit are twisted together to improve resistance to EMI

Shielded Twisted Pair (STP): two conductors of a circuit are twisted together to improve resistance to EMI and wrapped in an insulator material typically foil to create a shielding from external EMI

Single Core Coaxial: utilizes a single metal core, typically copper

Multi Core Coaxial: utilizes multiple metal strands

Single Mode Fiber: a fiber optic cable designed to carry a single transverse mode of light

Multi-Mode Fiber: a fiber optic cable typically used for short distances with a large core that enable multiple light modes to be propagated

Plenum Cable: electrical cabling that is laid in the plenum spaces, such as a raised floor or dropped ceiling of building, typically contains low smoke PVC jacket

Riser Cable: electrical cabling that is ran between floors and non-plenum areas.

Mesh Topology: a network model in which all devices are interconnected

Star Topology: a network model in which all devices are connected to a central node

Bus Topology: a network model in which all devices are connected to a single line or backbone

Network Access Control (NAC) devices

A computer security approach that implements a technical means for users or systems to authenticate to the network, typically enforces requirements on the endpoint devices by utilizing a HIPS or antivirus.

Endpoint security

A computer security process that protects network endpoint devices from threats, typically this is accomplished with a HIPS or antivirus. This security process could include compliance standards to ensure a baseline level of security to the network.

4.3 Implement secure communication channels according to design

---

Voice

There are a few different options for voice communication, the POTS system is what is typically referred to when talking about using the public telephone network, while a PBX can be used to create an internal only communication system and VOIP can be used to have your voice communications over the TCP/IP system, which can also handle an internal only network of communications.

Private Branch Exchange (PBX): a private telephony network, these systems traditionally utilized a private version of POTS, but has been modernized to use VOIP

Plain Old Telephone System (POTS): an analog signal transmission network that allowed for voice communications

Voice over Internet Protocol (VOIP): a technology that enable the use of voice calls over TCP/IP infrastructure, also called IP telephony.

Multimedia collaboration

Remote Meetings: this category includes tools such as Zoom, Microsoft Teams, Slack and Google Workspace, these are collaboration tools that allow for remote voice, video, file sharing and chat capabilities. A major consideration in the use of these technologies is the security of the meeting and ensuring that unauthorized users are not able to join.

Content Distribution Network (CDN): geographically separated servers that cache content and allow for end users to access multimedia content from the nearest server to their physical location, this allows for media content to be accessed more quickly by the client

Remote access

Point-to-Point Tunneling Protocol (PPTP): a method to create a VPN, uses port 1723, utilizes a TCP control channel and encapsulation to send Point-to-Point Protocol (PPP) packets, can use multiple authentication protocols such as MS-CHAP or RADIUS.

Layer Two Tunneling Protocol (L2TP): a method to create a VPN, uses UDP port 1701, encrypts only the control messages, creates a layer 2 tunnel between networks, typically paired with IPSEC to encrypt layer 3 traffic.

Internet Protocol Security (IPsec): a method to authenticate and encrypt layer 3 packets over an IP network, uses port 500

Secure Socket Tunneling Protocol (SSTP): a method to create a VPN, port can vary and be assigned, proprietary protocol released by Microsoft.

OpenVPN: a method to create a VPN, port can vary and be assign, open-source protocol that utilizes TLS encryption and allows for multiple authentication techniques such as certificates, username/password, or pre-shared keys (PSK).

Challenge Handshake Authentication Protocol (CHAP): an authentication mechanism uses in PPP, utilizes a three-way handshake to verify client

Microsoft CHAP (MS-CHAP): an authentication mechanism that is used in PPTP, RADIUS and PEAP, utilizes a challenge/response to verify clients, uses DES encryption and is vulnerable to attacks

Extensible Authentication Protocol (EAP): a network authentication framework that has multiple different implementations such as LEAP, TEAP, EAP PSAK and many more, EAP is primarily used in wireless technologies

Protected Extensible Authentication Protocol (PEAP): an encapsulation protocol that wraps EAP into a TLS tunnel.

Remote Authentication Dial-In User Service (RADIUS): a method for devices to be authenticated to a network that utilizes a Server that maintains a user database and Clients which are the networking devices such as switch's or routers which are used to authenticate users. Radius can be implemented with a VPN to ensure that only authorized devices/users are allowed into the network.

Microsoft Remote Desktop (RDP): a proprietary protocol developed by Microsoft for the sharing of a users desktop across a network that can be viewed and controlled by another user, uses port 3389

Secure Shell (SSH): a client/server remote command line cryptographic protocol that supports authentication by username/password or private key, supports tunneling, forwarding and remote desktop via X11.

Data communications

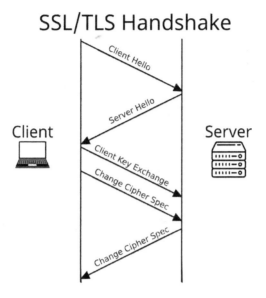

Secure Socket Layer (SSL): a security protocol used to establish an encrypted connection between a client and a server.

Transport Layer Security (TLS): a security protocol that replaced SSL used to establish an encrypted connection between a client and a server.

Secure Electronic Transaction (SET): a protocol for communicating electronic payment that was established in 1996, used to secure payments in e-commerce

Virtualized networks

Virtual Switch: a software implementation of a multi-layered switch that provides switching for virtual environments

Virtual Local Area Network (VLAN): a separate broadcast domain that exists logically at the data link layer and contains a grouping a of devices either physical or virtual

Software Defined Network (SDN): an approach to networking that enables different software to be installed on network hardware that can make the network more dynamic and efficient, the goal is to not be concerned with the underlying hardware and make the management and operation a simple process

Virtual eXtensible Local Area Network (VXLAN): a VLAN created in a virtual environment using software-defined (virtual) switches

Software-Defined Wide Area Network (SD-WAN): a virtual WAN architecture that allows enterprises to leverage any combination of transport services, including MPLS, LTE and broadband internet service, to securely connect users to applications

Third-party connectivity

It may be needed for a third party to be able to communicate to devices on an organizations internal network, in this case it is advised that the connection be monitored and that appropriate security measures are put in place to ensure that the connection does not compromise the network.

Domain 5: Identity and Access Management (IAM) (13%)

5.1 Control physical and logical access to assets

Information

Access controls permissions such as file and folder level permission to control what information users have access to. Information can also be contained in databases, and it is important to ensure that appropriate permissions are set for database tables.

Facilities

Defense in depth should guide the overall security posture of physical security into your facility. Think of your most physical assets as the inner layers of an onion with each layer becoming slightly less important or used as a mechanism to protect the next layer.

Fences, walls and gates can provide perimeter security and deter an intruder; however, it is important to ensure you have a detective mechanism to know if these boundaries have been crossed.

Security guards and sentries can patrol the facility to ensure that only authorized personnel are on the grounds.

Badge access can limit the movement and access that an unauthorized individual would be able to achieve.

Mantraps and sally ports will ensure that individuals and vehicles are not tailgating to gain access to areas they should not be allowed to access.

Escorts will ensure that guests to not wander to areas that they are not supposed to be, and additionally a visitor log will keep a record of all guests and who their accompanying escort was.

Systems

Physical access to computing systems such as desktops, laptops, tablets, smartphones, etc., should be restricted to personnel that are authorized to use the systems. And systems should be checked out when applicable to ensure physical accountability.

Logical access includes the ability to remotely access a system, and due care should be taken to ensure logical security by securing unused ports and making sure that installed programs have up to date security patches. Remote access should be encrypted by utilizing a VPN, and only authorized personnel should be able to log into systems remotely.

Applications

The ability for systems to run applications should be limited to applications that are trusted by an organization. It should also be considered that if a company has an application with an API the API should be secured to ensure that only authorized users are able to access the API and its functions.

Application Programming Interface (API): a piece of software that bridges communication of two different applications; allows access of an application programmatically by another application.

Devices

When devices are checked out to anyone a hand receipt should be accomplished and an acceptable use policy should be signed, employees should be adequately trained on security threats relating to mobile devices and security steps to physically secure their devices.

Certain devices should be prohibited from use on company computers and networks, devices such as removeable USB drives, cell phone chargers and personal electronic devices should not be allowed to interact with company hardware.

Wearable devices pose a potential security risk as they may contain wireless communications mechanisms such as WiFi and Bluetooth that could be used to launch exploits into a corporate network, the use of these devices should be determined by the sensitivity level of the computing systems and risk accepted by the organization.

5.2 Manage identification and authentication of people, devices, and services

Identity Management (IdM) implementation

Identity Management implementation is a constantly evolving landscape and is most likely no longer simply an Active Directory instance that control all the users on an enterprise, Identification, Authentication, Authorization, and Accountability (IAAA) are the fundamental building blocks for identity management.

Identification: presentation of user to a system, this is generally a user id or username.

Authentication: verification that the user is who they claim to be, usually with a pin or password

Authorization: verification of what the user is allowed to do or what data the user has access to.

Accountability: logging of the identification, authentication and authorization processes.

Single/Multi-Factor Authentication (MFA)

Authentication the process of presenting your pin, passcode, token to verify that you are who you claim to be, there are five types of authentications.

Type 1: What you know, password based.
Type 2: What you have, smart card, token.
Type 3: What you are, biometrics based.
Type 4: Where you are, location based.
Type 5: What you do, pattern based

Single Factor: uses only one of the five types of authentications

Multi-Factor: utilizes more than one of the five types of authentications

Accountability

Accountability is the principal that any violation or failed attempt at acquiring an identification or authorization needs to be logged, this creates a level of assurance that the system is being used as intended.

Session management

User sessions should be managed in a secure manner, this will often involve administrative policies that require users to lock their computers when leaving or stepping away. A technical solution that can help with session management is forced session teardown during night hours or session timeouts, this would ensure that users sessions are at a minimum reestablished every day.

Registration, proofing, and establishment of identity

Establishment: is the process of determining what that user's identity will be.
Proofing: is the act of ensuring that a person is who he claims to be
Registration: is the act of entering the identity into the IAM solution

Federated Identity Management (FIM)

A system that allows users to sign in with the same identifiers to separate enterprises, this is done by a user when a user attempts to login to one Service Provider (SP) and the SP then passes the requests to the Identity Provider (IdP), this is typically accomplished using SAML or OAUTH.

Credential Management Systems (CMS)

An important part of the PKI system, the credential management software is used to issue and manage certificates. CMS should implement a Hardware Security Module to ensure that certificates issued are valid and cryptographically secure.

Single Sign On (SSO)

An access methodology that allows a user to login with single authentication mechanism across multiple services, a true use of single sign on would allow the user to log in on any one service and use multiple services without needing to log in again.

Just-In-Time (JIT)

An access methodology that focuses on least privilege and requires users to justify or request access to a resource. This can be accomplished with ephemeral accounts and temporary elevation.

Ephemeral Accounts: these are one time use accounts, or temporary accounts that are given access and immediately deprovisioned

Temporary Elevation: a request is made to request elevated access to a resource, this is granted on a time-based basis, after time is up the access is removed.

5.3 Federated identity with a third-party service

On-premises

The utilization of an identity provider (IdP) that stores and verifies user identity that is utilized for on premise applications. This may be needed if your organization is running proprietary internal applications.

Cloud

The utilization of an identity provider (IdP) that stores and verifies user identity that is utilized for cloud applications, this model creates a quickly deployable and scalable solution for cloud-based applications.

Hybrid

The utilization of an identity provider (IdP) that stores and verifies user identity that is utilized for both on premise and cloud-based applications.

5.4 Implement and manage authorization mechanisms

Role Based Access Control (RBAC)

A security mechanism in which access is granted to users based on job roles or tasks to be accomplished

Rule based access control

A security mechanism in which access is granted to users based on a set of rules and policies

Mandatory Access Control (MAC)

A security mechanism by which the operating system or database constrains the ability of a subject, and their associated clearance, to access an object based on its classification

Discretionary Access Control (DAC)

A security mechanism that controls access as decided by the owner of the object.

Attribute Based Access Control (ABAC)

A security mechanism that *provides access to users based on who they are rather than what they do.*

Risk based access control

A non-static authentication system which considers the profile (IP address, User-Agent HTTP header, time of access) of the agent requesting access to the system to determine the risk profile associated with that transaction.

5.5 Manage the identity and access provisioning lifecycle

Account access review (e.g., user, system, service)

As part of account management and access control, accounts should be periodically reviewed to ensure users have accurate roles, right and privileges. This is most important for users that have long standing accounts as privilege creep can occur. It is also important to note this review should include all types of accounts to include system and service accounts.

User Account: while technically all accounts are user accounts, it is generally referred to as a user account if the account is being operated by a human

System Account: an account with escalated privileges, created by the operating system and runs operating system processes

Service Account: an account that is created for a service, this allows for security limitations to be placed on the account while giving it potentially more privileges than a user account

Provisioning and deprovisioning (e.g., on /off boarding and transfers)

A management process that will need to comply with corporate policies, this process deals with the creation and deletion of user accounts, part of deprovisioning could also happen during an interdepartmental transfer.

Role definition (e.g., people assigned to new roles)

Determining which roles are needed and which the associated permissions for the role.

Privilege escalation (e.g., managed service accounts, use of sudo, minimizing its use)

Privileged account management: mechanisms should be put in place to protect privileged accounts such as administrator, service, system and domain accounts, these accounts should be audited and reviewed more frequently than standard user accounts as set by company policy.

Managed Service Accounts: service accounts are used to run services, this allows for restriction of the service account to specific resources that the service needs, but typically service account passwords do not expire, it is important to carefully monitor and manage these accounts

superuser do (sudo): a program within unix type operating systems that allows a user to execute commands at the highest level of user security privileges, sudo use should be minimal in an organization and only admin accounts should be able to execute sudo, administrators should have normal user accounts that they conduct normal business on. The idea is that admin should have to switch from user to admin account and then have to run sudo.

Privilege Creep: the slow addition of privileges to user accounts, without removed unneeded or old permissions

Privilege Escalation: the ability to change from a standard user to a user with higher levels of permissions, this can be an ordinary administrative process, but it can also be used in the event of a breach to obtain administrative credentials.

5.6 Implement authentication systems

OpenID Connect (OIDC)/Open Authorization (Oauth)

Open Authorization (OAuth): an open standard that allows for SSO over HTTPS without the use of passwords, but rather utilizes access tokens to grant access

OpenID Connect (OIDC): a layer of identification that stacks on top of OAuth 2.0 that allows clients to confirm end user identity utilizing authentication via an authorization server.

Security Assertion Markup Language (SAML)

SAML is an open authentication standard, using Extensible Markup Language (XML) that web applications utilize to send authentication data between two parties, the identity provider (IdP) and the service provider (SP).

Kerberos

A single sign on (SSO) protocol that allows for network authentication over insecure networks with the use of tickets, named after Kerberos the three headed dog from Greek mythology, Kerberos has three basic elements, client authentication, client service authorization, client service request.

Client Authentication

1. The client sends a cleartext message of the user ID to the AS (Authentication Server) requesting services on behalf of the user.
2. The AS checks to see if the client is in its database. If it is, the AS generates the secret key by hashing the password of the user found at the database (e.g., Active Directory in Windows Server) and sends back the following two messages to the client:
    a. Message A: Client/TGS Session Key encrypted using the secret key of the client/user.
    b. Message B: Ticket-Granting-Ticket (TGT, which includes the client ID, client network address, ticket validity period, and the Client/TGS Session Key) encrypted using the secret key of the TGS.
3. Once the client receives messages A and B, it attempts to decrypt message A with the secret key generated from the password entered by the user. With a valid password and secret key the client decrypts message A to obtain the Client/TGS Session Key. This session key is used for further communications with the TGS. At this point, the client has enough information to authenticate itself to the TGS.

Client Service Authorization

1. When requesting services, the client sends the following messages to the TGS:
    a. Message C: Composed of the message B (the encrypted TGT using the TGS secret key) and the ID of the requested service.
    b. Message D: Authenticator (which is composed of the client ID and the timestamp), encrypted using the Client/TGS Session Key.
2. Upon receiving messages C and D, the TGS retrieves message B out of message C. It decrypts message B using the TGS secret key. This gives it the Client/TGS Session Key and the client ID (both are in the TGT). Using this Client/TGS Session Key, the TGS decrypts message D (Authenticator) and compares the client IDs from messages B and D; if they match, the server sends the following two messages to the client:

     a. Message E: Client-to-server ticket (which includes the client ID, client network address, validity period, and Client/Server Session Key) encrypted using the service's secret key.

     b. Message F: Client/Server Session Key encrypted with the Client/TGS Session Key.

Client Service Request

1. Upon receiving messages E and F from TGS, the client has enough information to authenticate itself to the Service Server (SS). The client connects to the SS and sends the following two messages:

     a. Message E: From the previous step (the Client-to-server ticket, encrypted using service's secret key).

     b. Message G: A new Authenticator, which includes the client ID, timestamp and is encrypted using Client/Server Session Key.

2. The SS decrypts the ticket (message E) using its own secret key to retrieve the Client/Server Session Key. Using the sessions key, SS decrypts the Authenticator and compares client ID from messages E and G, if they match server sends the following message to the client to confirm its true identity and willingness to serve the client:

     a. Message H: The timestamp found in client's Authenticator (plus 1 in version 4, but not necessary in version 5[9][10]), encrypted using the Client/Server Session Key.

3. The client decrypts the confirmation (message H) using the Client/Server Session Key and checks whether the timestamp is correct. If so, then the client can trust the server and can start issuing service requests to the server.

4. The server provides the requested services to the client.

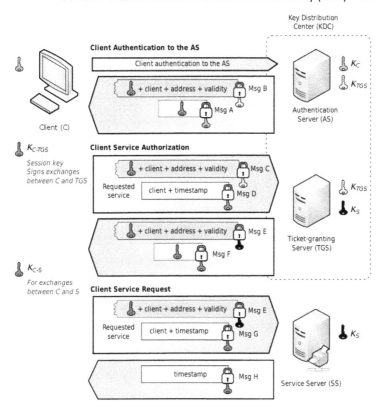

Remote Authentication Dial-In User Service (RADIUS)/Terminal Access Controller Access Control System Plus (TACACS+)

Remote Authentication Dial-In User Service (RADIUS): a service that authenticates, authorizes, and accounts for devices on a network, this provides security by protecting the network from unauthorized devices. Operates over UDP ports 1645 and 1812.

Terminal Access Controller Access Control System Plus (TACACS+): developed by Cisco TACACS+ provides authentication, authorization and accounting services, but does so fully encrypted. Operates on TCP port 49

Domain 6: Security Testing and Assessment (12%)

6.1 Design and validate assessment, test, and audit strategies

The first step in creating an assessment program is to ensure that it is designed to fully test every scenario and that the logging system is sufficient. Audits should be designed in such a way as to ensure accountability to policy and not just adding an administrative burden that does not signal when there is a problem.

Internal

Internal audit is typically performed by the company using its own resources. The purpose of internal audit is to regularly check various business systems for compliance with policies and procedures.

External

Initiated by a company to review its own security protocols by engaging an outside audit company.

Third-party

In third-party audits, an independent body or entity that is not affiliated with the company conducts the audit. Can be initiated by regulatory bodies. Can examine both internal and external auditors.

Third party audits can also refer to ensuring that you have policy in place to audit third parties that require connection into you network, this can occur when a vendor contracts another party to fulfill part of their obligations.

6.2 Conduct security control testing

Vulnerability assessment

Vulnerability assessment is the process of identifying risk inside a network, once risk has been identified the vulnerabilities can be ranked in order of importance and a report is generated giving leadership a picture of the state of the computer network for an organization.

Security Content Automation Protocol (SCAP): is a method for using specific standards to enable automated vulnerability management, measurement, and policy compliance evaluation of systems deployed in an organization, including, FISMA compliance.

Penetration testing

Penetration testing goes further than vulnerability assessment, as the goal of penetration testing is to exploit vulnerabilities that are found. This type of testing can occur with or without the knowledge of the network defense teams depending on the desired outcome. Penetration testing will closely resemble the cyber kill chain, possibly skipping a few steps depending on if conducting a black, grey or white box test.

Black Box: attacks are done from the outsider or hacker perspective, no information is provided to the penetration test team, simulates a realistic threat

Grey Box: testers have some knowledge, may have some reconnaissance data provided or a user account, this methodology allows for cost savings, but still gives a good idea of realistic vulnerabilities inside a network.

White Box: attackers have detailed knowledge of the network, may be provided an admin account or foothold in the network, bypasses lengthy reconnaissance phase, but has potential to miss critical steps

Modified Cyber Kill Chain:

1. **Reconnaissance:** during this phase the attacker will conduct open-source research, such as getting company email schemas, and finding available vulnerabilities
2. **Exploitation:** perform exploitation of vulnerabilities identified during recon phase, can be exploiting service or social engineering mechanism
3. **Privilege Escalation:** if not already on an admin account, attackers will attempt to gain admin access
4. **Lateral Movement:** move laterally within the corporation, with an end state to gain access to a protected network segment or gain access to data
5. **Exfiltration/Goal:** this step identifies if that attacker was successfully able to gain access to the agreed upon end state, be it take full control of network, make a domain account, or VLAN hop to protected network
6. **Report:** the main goal of pen testing is to reveal vulnerabilities on the network, this is accomplished with a final report that is delivered to the customer

Log reviews

Logs that are not reviewed are somewhat pointless, logs are always going to be only able to detect an attack after the fact, but even after the fact, attacks can only be detected if an effective strategy is in place to utilize logs to find abnormalities in the network.

Syslog: a standard for logging that separates the role of the system generating, the system that stores and the system that analyzes the logs. This is typically operated over a network with a client-server relationship, a network can have a syslog server setup with many client feeding logs to the server. The recorded logs are typically fed into a Secure Information and Event Management (SIEM) server for further analysis.

Traffic Analysis: the process of intercepting and inspecting network traffic, the metadata and packet data may be recorded and sent into a Secure Information and Event Management (SIEM) server, allowing for analysts to search through and correlate network data.

Secure Information and Event Management (SIEM): a server/software that collects information form network traffic and hosts to provide real time security alerts and allowing for further analysis by analysts.

Synthetic transactions

Synthetic transactions, or synthetic monitoring, involves building scripts or tools that simulate activities normally performed in an application, a good synthetic transaction will appear as a human performing the tasks.

Misuse case testing

The process of testing by entering incorrect information on forms or fields, this could also utilize fuzzing.

Fuzzing: an automated software that enters incorrect, unexpected, or random data into a software application, while analyzing the software application for faults, such as memory leaks, open ports, crashes or exposing memory for exploit.

Test coverage analysis

A mathematical approach to determining if a program has been thoroughly tested, yielding a percentage. This requires that you find all possible use cases for a given program, this can prove difficult as it can be almost impossible to predict or gather all possible use cases, especially for a complex program.

test coverage = (use cases tested / total use cases)

Interface testing

A typical programming team will work on different modules of a software product, interface testing is conducted to ensure that the modules operate according to specification provided to the developer, and ultimately all the modules operate together properly without any flaws.

Application Programming Interface (API): a piece of software that bridges communication of two different applications; a perfect example of modular programming is the use of APIs. APIs typically contain multiple modules that are used by developers to conduct many different types of actions.

Breach attack simulations

Automated platform designed to simulate behaviors that closely resemble real-world threat actions in order to determine whether they are detected by your security controls

Compliance checks

On the spot reviews to ensure compliance, this is different than audits which check compliance over a specific time period.

Code review and testing

Code review is a process to test software before is released into a production environment, this typically includes testing performance, reliability, and security of an application.

Static: evaluates software without running the code, source code is inspected, or application processed through a decompiler to get machine level instructions.

Dynamic: evaluates the behavior of software once it has been executed, this is best accomplished in a sandbox, with minimal software running and recording tools tracking processes, file actions and network traffic. This type of testing may utilize synthetic transaction to interact with the software.

6.3 Collect security process data (e.g., technical and administrative)

Account management

Account Escalation: the process of additional privileges being added when a user changes roles in an organization, it is important to make sure that the permissions are evaluated to ensure the user is not retaining permissions that are no longer required.

Account Revocation: the process in which a user access is revoked, it is important to note that deleting an account may also remove access to data created by the user, rather than deleting the account it should be disabled for a period then deleted.

Management review and approval

A review and approval process should be implanted and mandated to ensure an effective security process. The review process should be scheduled to ensure that management and administrators have the opportunity to approve security recommendations before they become critical breaches.

Key performance and risk indicators

Utilizing industry standards such as NIST standards it is important for an organization to have and understanding of its KRI and KPI to ensure that the organization is meeting its goals
assd and no
t overly exposing itself to risk.

Key Risk Indicators (KRI): an indicator used by management as a metric to determine the level of risk for a given activity

Key Performance Indicators (KPI): an indicator used by management to determine the success of an organization in moving towards a given goal

NIST SP800-137 — Information Security Continuous Monitoring (ISCM) for Federal Information Systems and Organizations

NIST SP800-137 — Risk Management Framework for Information Systems and Organizations: A System Life Cycle Approach for Security and Privacy

NIST Cybersecurity Framework - Framework for Improving Critical Infrastructure Cybersecurity

Backup verification data

It is important that an organization has a data backup plan in place, included in that plan should be all the data used to verify the security posture of the organization. The security process is iterative and each time the systems are assessed those assessments should be backed up.

Training and awareness

Training and security awareness is possibly one of the most important ways to prevent a data breach, but this is reliant on current and up to date training. The training and awareness plan for users should be updated based on the current threats and risks to an organization and should evolve based on the effectiveness of previous trainings and evaluations.

Disaster Recovery (DR) and Business Continuity (BC)

A disaster can be devastating to any organization, and during disaster recovery or business continuity operations security is often overlooked or left out entirely in an chaotic attempt to restore business operations. Security needs to be a part of the disaster recovery planning process to ensure that in the event of a disaster, there is a plan in place. *If security is not in a disaster plan before a disaster, you can plan on security being part of the disaster.*

Disaster Recovery (DR): an organizations response and ability to cope with a disaster that has negatively impacted business operations.

Business Continuity (BC): an organizations ability to continue operations in the wake of a disaster and return to normal operations.

6.4 Analyze test output and generate report

Remediation

Reporting should contain remediation solutions to the vulnerabilities that were identified. This part of the report should be kept internal and protected from external release as it would provide sensitive information about flaws in the network. The remediation section of the report should include references to the vulnerability such as the CVE and it should include detailed steps for the proposed remediation solution.

Exception handling

The process of introducing errors into a system to ensure and determine that the system can handle the errors in a secure manner

Ethical disclosure

Once a system has been evaluated and a final report has been generated there is an ethical requirement to release to information to your shareholders, investors and the public. The amount of information required for each party is different and to make it simple there are different type 1 and type 2 tests that are defined, and different Service Organization Controls (SOC) reports targeting for the different audiences.

Service Organization Control (SOC):

- Type 1: Evaluates design
- Type 2: Evaluates design and effectiveness
- SOC 1: intended for financial auditors and investors
- SOC 2: intended for internal use by IT staff, regulators etc
- SOC 3: intended for public as a pass/fail summary of SOC 2

	Type 1: Design of Controls	Type 2: Control Design & Effectiveness
SOC 1: Report for Financial Auditors and Investors		
SOC 2: Internal Report for Assessing Internal Controls		
SOC 3: Public Pass/Fail Summary of SOC 2		

6.5 Conduct or facilitate security audits

Security audits should be conducted according to the design and plan that has been approved.

Internal

Internal audit is typically performed by the company using its own resources. The purpose of internal audit is to regularly check various business systems for compliance with policies and procedures.

External

Initiated by a company to review its own security protocols by engaging an outside audit company.

Third-party

In third-party audits, an independent body or entity that is not affiliated with the company conducts the audit. Can be initiated by regulatory bodies. Can examine both internal and external auditors

Third party audits can also refer to ensuring that you have policy in place to audit third parties that require connection into you network, this can occur when a vendor contracts another party to fulfill part of their obligations.

Domain 7: Security Operations (13%)

7.1 Understand and comply with investigations

Evidence collection and handling

!!! Always Secure the Scene !!!

Evidence Lifecycle:
- **Identification and collection**: data is collected
- **Examination**: pertinent data is examined
- **Report:** report finding to prosecution
- **Presented:** evidence is presented in court

Locard's Principle: The principal that every contact leaves a trace, and an exchange of material. This means that with contact you will both take something and leave something.

Live Evidence: evidence such as RAM that will be lost if the system is shutdown

Chain of Custody: the process of documenting who has control over evidence, to ensure that it has not been

Discovery: legal process that allows parties to inquire about evidence from the other side in relation to the case

eDiscovery: digital investigation that is looking for digital evidence

Digital: evidence that is binary form

Physical: evidence that is tangible

Biological: evidence that contains DNA

Direct: evidence that proves a face

5 rules of evidence:
- Admissible – able to be used in court
- Authentic – evidence is relevant to the incident
- Complete – not one sided, includes exculpatory evidence
- Reliable – collection practices cannot cause doubt
- Believable – understandable to everyone, jury can believe

Reporting and documentation

An investigative report should be accomplished, and all evidence should be well documented to show the most likely series of events.

Investigative techniques

Interviewing: a technique used to investigate is conducting interviews, during the interview it is important to be respectful, this technique is often used to get witness statements or determine firsthand how an incident happened, unless acted in a law enforcement role this is a completely optional on the part of the subject

Forensics: a technique used to investigate is gathering forensic evidence, in terms of digital incidents, this is often getting logs, memory captures and images of hard disks, forensic data is typically time sensitive and should be collected quickly and with due care

Surveillance: a technique used to investigate is surveillance, this is watching a subject that you suspect committed an offense and you are either trying to gather incriminating evidence or potentially if they repeat the offense, this can take place in the form of monitoring a user's computer usage, this likely will involve a user agreement to be monitored

Means: tools and capability

Motive: a reason

Opportunity: being present at the time of the incident

Means + Motive + Opportunity = Suspect

Digital forensics tools, tactics, and procedures

Tools: the software used by security professionals to obtain or recover digital forensics, this is "what" you use to accomplish the job

Tactics: the "when and where" of using the tools

Procedures: the step-by-step instructions on "how" to use the tools

Common Forensics Tools:
- FTK Imager – create a image of a disk
- Sleuth-Kit – forensic analysis of images
- Volatility – Memory forensics
- Registry recon –rebuild windows registry from disk image
- Wireshark – packet level network analysis
- SIFT – Linux OS with preloaded forensic tools
- ExifTool - reads metadata of many different types of files

Types of Digital Forensics
- **Disk:** recovering deleted data from disk
- **Network:** network traffic and log files
- **Memory:** analysis of volatile data
- **Malware:** analyzing malicious software, attribution
- **Mobile:** analysis of mobile devices for evidence
- **Image:** analysis of metadata to determine authenticity

Types of investigation:
- **Criminal:** suspected of breaking criminal law (results: jail)
- **Civil:** suspected of being civilly liable (results: lawsuit)
- **Regulatory:** suspected of breaking regulations (results: fines)

• **Administrative:** suspected of breaking policy (results: admin)

Artifacts (e.g., computer, network, mobile device)

        Artifacts are pieces of evidence that are left from information systems interacting with each other, a common example would be logs that show a computer connected to the network. Common artifacts are registry keys, files, time stamps, router or switch logs, FW logs, IDS or IPS logs, system logs and metadata.

7.2 Conduct logging and monitoring activities

Intrusion detection and prevention

Intrusion Detection System (IDS): a network monitoring system, that can be in/out of band, this type of system looks for network traffic that matches signatures, when there is a match, it creates an alert/log entry

Intrusion Prevention System (IPS): a network monitoring system, that can only operate in-band, this system looks for network traffic that matches signatures, when there is a match the system blocks the network traffic from entering/leaving the network depending on the rule.

Security Information and Event Management (SIEM)

        A server/software that collects information form network traffic and hosts to provide real time security alerts and allowing for further analysis by analysts.

Continuous monitoring

A real time system that detects compliance and security issues, this system is in place permanently to ensure continuous coverage of the network.

Egress monitoring

The process of Egress Monitoring, also called Egress filtering, is when outbound traffic is monitored and possibly restricted; this is mostly used on protected networks, or to filter what data is allowed outbound from servers.

Log management

The approach used to administer large volumes of logs, this should be detailed in policy to include retention, aggregation, storage and collection of logs.

Threat intelligence (e.g., threat feeds, threat hunting)

Threat intelligence allows for systems such as your IDS or IPS to provide a benefit, without current threat intelligence these systems will not be able to alert/block any current or relevant threats.

Threat Feeds: a source of threat intelligence that is provided by an entity that constantly monitors malicious IP addresses, domains and behavior of threat actors. Feeds are generally provided directly to firewalls, IDS or IPS by utilizing a protocol such as STIX/TAXII.

Structured Threat Information eXpression: developed by MITRE and CTI used to describe threat information.

Trusted Automated eXchange of Intelligence Information: the technical methodology which allows the sharing of STIX data shared by services or messaging.

Threat Hunting: a proactive approach to cyber security, rather than waiting for news of a breach, threat hunting utilizes intelligence to look for malicious actors that may already be in a network that have not yet been discovered.

User and Entity Behavior Analytics (UEBA)

A security practice that requires obtaining a "normal" look at how users interact and behave on the network and utilizing an analytical, typically machine learning, that is capable of spotting behavior that is anomalous.

7.3 Perform Configuration Management (CM) (e.g., provisioning, baselining, automation)

Provisioning: process of setting up IT infrastructure, includes setting up authentication mechanisms for devices to access the network, once provisioned, the next step is configuration

Baselining: process of documenting the attributes of a configuration item (device) at a point in time, which serves as a basis for defining change

Automation is a feature in a configuration management tool that allows an administrator to quickly manage configuration items, including provisioning a new server within minutes with less room for error

7.4 Apply foundational security operations concepts

Need-to-know/least privilege

Need to know and least privilege can be mistaken for the same thing, be careful as they are not.

Least Privilege: the concept that users/system are only given access to what they need to complete their job, no more or less, exactly what they need

Need to Know: the concept that even if you are given access, if you don't need to know, you should not access the information

Separation of Duties (SoD) and responsibilities

The concept of separation of duties is used to prevent fraud and error, this is accomplishing by requiring more than one person to complete a task. This can be seen in the Clark Wilson model and the Chinese Wall model.

Privileged account management

Mechanisms put in place to protect privileged accounts such as administrator, service, system and domain accounts, these accounts should be audited and reviewed more frequently than standard user accounts as set by company policy.

Job rotation

A concept that requires a company to implement via policy in which employees are rotated to different positions to prevent fraud. This can be implemented by creating a

duty that trained employees are rotated through
on a time basis throughout the year, it is
possible with this type of policy to rotate
through a fixed number of trained employees.

Service Level Agreements (SLAs)

Service Level Requirement (SLR): requirements
for a service from the customers point of view

Service Level Agreement (SLA): agreement
between IT service provider and customer to
guarantee a service or performance level.
Penalties for failure are spelled out in the
contract

Service Level Report: insight into a service
provider ability to deliver the agreed upon
service quality.

7.5 Apply resource protection

Media management

The process used to maintain media
utilized within an organization, this can
include versioning, storage and backup of
installation media, license keys, hardware, and
code repositories.

**Information Technology Infrastructure Library
(ITIL):** a collection of precise methods for
optimizing information technology asset
management by increasing efficiency, decreasing
risk, and boosting security

1. improving IT efficiency
2. reducing IT related risk
3. enhancing IT security

Media protection techniques

Media protection techniques should be deployed to ensure that all forms of media are secured, including magnetic hard drives, solid state drives, flash drives, DVDs, and tapes. Security professionals should ensure that the appropriate media protection policies and procedures are documented for media on all device types, including computers, mobile devices, and network hardware. When in storage media should be encrypted and physical access should be limited.

Overwriting: a process to reuse the physical disk by overwriting all the data on the disk, this is not secure as data can still typically be recovered in a lab, and should only be used for use in the same classification as original data

Purging: a process in which data is removed from the disk in a way that data will not be able to be recovered, disk is not intended for reuse

Degaussing: a process that destroys magnetic media only, this is done by exposing the media to a strong magnetic field, disk is not intended for reuse, does not work on Solid State Drives

Destruction: a process that the physical disk is destroyed and is no longer readable rendering it incapable of storing data, this is done by disk crushers, shredders, incinerating, pulverizing and acid.

Crypto Shredding: a process in which the data is stored encrypted on a disk and the encryption key is permanently destroyed or deleted, this can be useful in cloud, or third party hosted environments

7.6 Conduct incident management

Incident management: the management of activities to detect, analyze, respond to, and correct an organization's security after a breach to its network has occurred.

Detection

This is possibly one of the most difficult steps, most breaches in security are not discovered for weeks, months and years if they are detected at all. This step requires that you find a security incident that has happened.

Response

There is no "one size fits all" solution when talking about responding to security breaches. In some instances, it might be worth allowing the adversary to continue their activities while you monitor what they are doing. In most circumstances companies will choose to remove the intruder. Regardless it is important to capture all available volatile data and track forensic data both past and present.

Mitigation

As the name of the step suggests the goal is to mitigate any further damage, this can only be done once you understand a) how the attacker got into your network b) what they have done once inside your network.

Reporting

Reporting is required to fully understand the scope of what has happened and inform management, so that informed decisions can be made providing a way forward.

Recovery

After management approval eradication steps are taken to completely restore the systems to a working state without the presence of the attacker, this step requires that all necessary patches and safeguards are put in place to proceed operations.

Remediation

The process of securing or hardening the system to ensure that the attacker does not return, and that the system does not suffer from similar attacks on the network

Lessons learned

A crucial step that often gets overlooked, is documenting, and reporting on faults and problems, this is often looking for a root cause of the problem and attempts to provide solutions to that problem. This is often represented in the form of a report that is given to management.

7.7 Operate and maintain detective and preventative measures

Firewalls (e.g., next generation, web application, network)

Next Generation Firewall (NGFW): a third-generation firewall that combines a traditional stateful firewall, with a web application firewall and an Intrusion Prevention System (IPS). NGFW's are located in-line and utilize deep packet inspection to inspect protocols being used, not just looking at ports, they

also typically utilize threat feeds to ensure
they are blocking current threats.

Web Application Firewall (WAF): a very specific
type of firewall that is looking at web traffic
and services, these firewalls can be hardware,
software or cloud based.

Network: security devices that protects a
network, based on defined security rules,
typically used at network boundaries to control
the flow of traffic in/out of the network.

Intrusion Detection Systems (IDS) and Intrusion Prevention Systems (IPS)

Intrusion Detection System (IDS): a network
monitoring system, that can be in/out of band,
this type of system looks for network traffic
that matches signatures or behavior, when there
is a match, it creates an alert/log entry

Intrusion Prevention System (IPS): a network
monitoring system, that can only operate in-
band, this system looks for network traffic
that matches signatures, when there is a match,
the system blocks the network traffic from
entering/leaving the network depending on the
rule.

Signature: a rule that is based on known
threats

Behaviors: a rule that is based on general
knowledge of how an attack is performed, can
detect unknown signatures

Whitelisting/blacklisting

Whitelist: a system used on both network and
host devices that specify an implicit allow to
a certain domain or piece of software, this
type of system will typically not allow any

other traffic or software other than what is on the whitelist.

Blacklist: a system used on both network and host devices that specify an implicit deny to a certain domain or piece of software, this system allows all traffic or software that is not on the blacklist and requires the blacklist to be updated with current threats.

Third-party provided security services

An external entity that provides security on a contractual basis.

Sandboxing

The use of a system that is isolated from any network, that mimics a production system, used to test software rollout or to run malware in a controlled environment.

Honeypots/honeynets

Honeypot: an isolated system that is purposefully vulnerable, set up to attract an adversary, once exploited the adversaries' behaviors are monitored to better understand methodology of a threat actor

Honeynet: an isolated network of systems that is purposefully vulnerable, set up as bait to attract an adversary, once exploited the adversaries' behaviors are monitored, this type of system generally will resemble a real corporate network and have fake data setup to be exfiltrated.

Anti-malware

A piece of software that analyzes executed programs within a system to determine if the program is safe to run. Anti-malware software utilizes signatures and heuristics to protect a host system.

Machine learning and Artificial Intelligence (AI) based tools

Tools that don't require any human interaction, can adapt to changes, operate at scale, and reproduce cognitive abilities to automate tasks.

Machine Learning: a statistical approach to data that allows a machine to analyze large data set to "learn" what "normal" looks like and find anomalous data, this works best for very specific tasks.

Artificial Intelligence: an overarching term to describe the different technologies that learn, and act based on inputs provided or derived, mostly what we have available is assistive intelligence, which improves tasks that we are already doing at a much larger scale.

7.8 Implement and support patch and vulnerability management

Patch and vulnerability management is a process used to control the release and installation of patches throughout an enterprise. This is a formal process that is intended to assess, test, install and verify patches before they are installed throughout the enterprise.

Common Patch Management Steps:

- **Download vendor patches:** patches are released sporadically and at different time from different vendors, it is important to have a comprehensive asset list and ensure that you are checking available patches consistently.

- **Testing of Patches:** patches should first be installed on a non-production system to ensure that everything functions, and no unforeseen issues are encountered.
- **Distribution of Patches:** there should be a policy as to when patches are installed on the enterprise to ensure that there is little to no downtime, also that a system is in place to push patches to systems throughout the network. Additionally, a process should be in place to quarantine systems from the network that reach a threshold of non-compliance.
- **Rollback Capabilities:** any patch management plan should contain the possibility that the patches installed will have negative repercussions and be able to undo/uninstall the patches.
- **Reporting:** a rolling report should be maintained that details the compliance of systems throughout the network

---

7.9 Understand and participate in change management processes

Change management is a process used to control modifications that are made to a production environment, these modifications can be simple configuration changes or full architecture changes. This is a formal process set by company policy to request, design, test, review, approve, implement, and keep record of all modifications to the company networks.

Common Organization Change Management Steps:

- Identify/Request for Change: during this phase you would figure out a change that might be needed and request that the change be made, this could also include a proposal in the request
- Review/Approval for Change: a committee would review and assess the requested changes for feasibility, cost, impacted systems and rollback plans, afterwards the committee votes.
- Develop/Test the change: if approved the proposed change would need to be developed, tested and verified on a non-production environment to ensure that the changes do not have unforeseen consequences.
- Notification/Implementation: during this phase notification might be sent out making users aware of a change and any expected

downtimes, the changes would be performed, and an all-clear message would be sent after changes were made.
- Roll Back: this phase is a contingency that is setup in case there are errors or the change causes faults inside the network
- Final Report: a report should be generated detailing the steps that were taken to make the change, any errors or problems that were encountered and the final results.

7.10 Implement recovery strategies

Backup storage strategies

Offsite Storage: data storage that is not present within an organization

Data Replication: process of having data constantly backed up or mirrored to an alternative storage location, often used in hot sites

Incremental: back up any files that have changed since the last incremental or full backup

Differential: back up any files that have changed since the last full backup

Full Backup: back up all files, regardless of last time data was backed up

Recovery site strategies

Cold Sites: an alternative location that may contain some hardware, but nothing is configured

Warm Sites: an alternative location that contains hardware that is in place and configured, a backup is present for use when site is ready to go live

Hot Sites: an alternative site that is fully functional and ready to go live, these sites will often be mirror sites with failover capabilities.

Multiple processing sites

A version of having a hot site, having multiple facilities that operate as mirrors, this is frequently used for separate geographic regions when high availability and speed are a concern, these sites can also be load balanced.

System resilience, High Availability (HA), Quality of Service (QoS), and fault tolerance

System resilience: how resilient a system is to withstand a major disruption without total failure.

High Availability (HA): a given period in which a system is able to operate continuously without failure, this is used in a contractual agreement assuring uptimes.

Quality of Service (QoS): a benchmark measuring the performance of a service overall

Fault Tolerance: ability for a part or component to fail, but the system does not

7.11 Implement Disaster Recovery (DR) processes

Response

The first step in Disaster Recovery is always going to be respond. This is based on the initial assessment of damage and the type of disaster. The response to a disaster should be based off a disaster recovery plan in which

steps should be provided to ensure that nothing
is missed or left out during the initial
response to events. How you first react and
responds to a disaster will set the tone for
how you are able to recover.

Personnel

Processes should be established to
protect the most important asset that any
business has, its people. This should include
evacuation plans, first aid and all necessary
emergency supplies. Evacuation drills should be
conducted regularly so that in the event of an
actual emergency personnel are familiar with
where to go. First aid kits should be located
throughout the facility with signs indicating
where they are visible. Emergency supplies such
as fire extinguishers, fire blankets, escape
ladders, emergency rations should be present if
a shelter in place order is issued.

Communications

Emergency communications should be
established, communications between disaster
recovery teams and planning team are vital to
recovering from an emergency. This is one of
the most important physical assets in an
emergency.

Assessment

Damage is assessed and the overall safety
of buildings and equipment is inspected. This
phase also looks at the impact to services and
systems.

Restoration

All needed actions are taken to restore
normal operations.

Training and awareness

All employees should be trained and aware of the companies' steps and procedures that should be taken in the event of an emergency, this includes continuity of operations.

Lessons learned

A crucial step that often gets overlooked, is documenting, and reporting on faults and problems, this is often looking for a root cause of the problem and attempts to provide solutions to that problem. This is often represented in the form of a report that is given to management.

7.12 Test Disaster Recovery Plans (DRP)

BCP and DRP

1. Umbrella Approach
2. Escalation Approach
3. Departmental Approach

Read-through/tabletop

Read-through: a review of the DRP is done and the disaster recovery team must read through all the steps and procedures of the plan.

Tabletop: slightly more involved than a readthrough each team steps through the plan and submits inputs as to any issues or ways to improve the plan.

Walkthrough

The disaster team physically shows the steps that they would take according to the

DRP, they do not perform the actions physically, still a verbal walkthrough.

Simulation

The disaster in simulated and the disaster recovery team simulate following the DRP showing and demonstrating the actions they would take according to the DRP

Parallel

Recovery operations are performed at a mirror site or on a non-production network.

Full interruption

Recovery operations are performed on the live operational network.

7.13 Participate in Business Continuity (BC) planning and exercises

Business continuity is a strategy that is utilized to attempt to continue operations with minimal impact during a disaster. Business continuity requires that you have a dedicated team to identify core mission critical processes, prioritize recovery of critical processes, set recovery time and point objectives as well as creating dedicated disaster recovery plans. Once a disaster strikes business continuity will require a communication plan that allows communication with key leadership and personnel, additionally coordination with external emergency departments may be required.

Business Impact Analysis: the process in which key critical business function are identified and proper safeguards are put in place to increase operational resilience.

Recovery Time Objective (RTO): the amount of time required to restore critical business functions

Recovery Point Objective (RPO): a goal that is set for how recent the nearest backup point should be for being able to restore operations from that backup

Maximum Tolerable Downtime (MTD): the point of no return, this is the amount of time that a business function is down that it will create irreversible consequences. The MTD is equal to the RTO and the RTO combined.

Work Recovery Time (WRT): this is the amount of time needed to recover the system and verify data integrity.

Mean Time to Recovery (MTTR): average amount of time needed to recover from system failure or downtime

Mean Time Between Failure (MTBF): average amount of time between system/device failure

7.14 Implement and manage physical security

Perimeter security controls

Fences, walls, and gates can provide perimeter security and deter an intruder; however, it is important to ensure you have a detective mechanism to know if these boundaries have been crossed.
Security guards and sentries can patrol the facility to ensure that only authorized personnel are on the grounds.

Access Control: the application of a single point of entry, a means to ensure that all personnel must enter through a single point

such as visitor center, guard shack or
reception.

Live Monitoring: the application of cameras and
sensors being monitored by guards that can
respond to alarms or alerts, potentially
patrolling the premises

Internal security controls

Badge access can limit the movement and
access that an unauthorized individual would be
able to achieve.
Mantraps and sally ports will ensure that
individuals and vehicles are not tailgating to
gain access to areas they should not be allowed
to access.

7.15 Address personnel safety and security concerns

!!! **Human life is always Top Priority** !!!

Travel

It is necessary for employees to travel
for business, and during those travels they may
be put at increased risk. It is also possible
to increase the risk to the organization if
they have data with them. There are a few
things to keep in mind for personnel safety
during business travels:

- Be alert when staying at a hotel and don't open the door to people you don't know
- Be mindful of scams that used on travelers
- If travelling internationally be aware that fire safety standards and emergency phone numbers are not the same everywhere
- Free WiFi is often open and vulnerable to MiTM attacks
- If travelling with company data, ensure that it is encrypted while at rest and while being used.

Emergency management

Every organization should have emergency management plans in place, these plans should hold the safety and security of personnel as the priority. Emergency management plans should include natural and man-made disasters, and plans should be different based on the type of disaster that is likely to be encountered.

Security training and awareness

Employees should have regularly scheduled safety briefings about hazards that exist in the workplace and should be adequately trained on any safety equipment that is present in the workplace such as an eye wash station or fire extinguishers. In addition to keeping employees safe, it should be a part of the training how to keep company data secure in the event of an emergency.

Duress

In the event that an employee is in duress there should be a system in place that covertly allows them to alert others without compromising their own safety, such as a panic button, code word or a duress PIN. A good example is airline pilots use transponder code 7500 to signal hijacking. These systems are most common when there are large amounts of money, valuables, or a perception of an easy target.

Domain 8: Software Development (11%)

Development methodologies (e.g., Agile, Waterfall, DevOps, DevSecOps)

Waterfall: sequential software development process, that flows toward conclusion

SCRUM: a framework utilizing a flexible mindset

AGILE: a set of practices intended to improve the effectiveness of software development utilizing continuous improvement and adaptive planning.

Development and Operations (DevOps): a software development practice that combines software development with operations in order to shorten the development lifecycle

Development, Security and Operations (DevSecOps): a software development practice that combines software development with security and operations in order to shorten the development lifecycle while keeping security "baked in" to the software from inception

Maturity models (e.g., Capability Maturity Model (CMM), Software Assurance Maturity Model (SAMM))

Capability Mature Model (CMM): a process level improvement training and appraisal program

1. Level 1: Initial — processes are unpredictable, poorly defined

2. Level 2: managed/repeatable — processes are established for project but still reactive
3. level 3: defined: processes are established for the whole organized based on standards (proactive)
4. level 4: quantitatively managed: processes are measured and controlled
5. level 5: optimizing: there is a focus on continuous process improvement

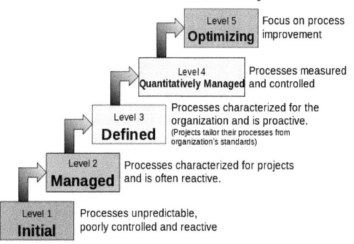

Characteristics of the Maturity levels

Level 5 Optimizing — Focus on process improvement

Level 4 Quantitatively Managed — Processes measured and controlled

Level 3 Defined — Processes characterized for the organization and is proactive. (Projects tailor their processes from organization's standards)

Level 2 Managed — Processes characterized for projects and is often reactive.

Level 1 Initial — Processes unpredictable, poorly controlled and reactive

Software Assurance Maturity Model (SAMM): an open framework created by OWASP designed to align specific risks of an organization to the software security posture.

SAMM v1.5

Business functions	Governance	Design	Implementation	Verification	Operations
Security practices	**Strategy & Metrics**	**Threat Assessment**	**Secure Build**	**Architecture Assessment**	**Incident Management**
	Create & promote / Measure & improve	Application risk profile / Threat modeling	Build process / Software dependencies	Architecture validation / Architecture compliance	Incident detection / Incident response
	Policy & Compliance	**Security Requirements**	**Secure Deployment**	**Requirements-driven Testing**	**Environment Management**
	Policy & standards / Compliance management	Software requirements / Supplier security	Deployment process / Secret management	Control verification / Misuse/abuse testing	Configuration hardening / Patch & update
	Education & Guidance	**Secure Architecture**	**Defect Management**	**Security Testing**	**Operational Management**
	Training & awareness / Organization & culture	Architecture design / Technology management	Defect tracking / Metrics & feedback	Scalable baseline / Deep understanding	Data protection / Legacy management
	Stream A / Stream B	Stream A / Stream B	Stream A / Stream B	Stream A / Stream B	Stream A / Stream B

Operation and maintenance

This phase of the SDLC is to ensure that software deployed is fully functioning and that it continues to function until it meets its end of life date.

Change management

Change management is a process used to control modifications that are made to a production environment, these modifications can be simple configuration changes or full architecture changes. This is a formal process set by company policy to request, design, test, review, approve, implement, and keep record of all modifications to the company networks.

Integrated Product Team (IPT)

A team comprised of appropriate disciplines relating to a project to maximize productivity, mostly used to solve complex problems that benefit from inputs of multiple disciplines.

8.2 Identify and apply security controls in software development ecosystems

To ensure that development environments remain secure they should be protected in the same manner as production networks, but they should remain separate networks that are isolated from each other, additionally the development network should have limited if any connection to the internet. No live customer or business data should be utilized in the development process and all activity in the network should be logged. Source code should be kept in secure repositories that exist only in the development network and cannot be accessed by anyone other than authorized developers.

Programming languages

Functional Programming: a programming design that is centered around the use of functions, sections of code that are called and can be easily repeated.

Object Oriented Programming (OOP): a programming design that is centered on the creation of objects, this is done by using classes to create an object blueprint. The blueprint can contain data or methods, objects can then be instantiated using the class blueprint and used as data objects.

Encapsulation: data inside objects is encapsulated by the object as defined by the private class that defined it, data is only accessible through public methods and public classes.

Abstraction: used to hide background data that is not needed by the user

Polymorphism: allows different objects to be handled by single interfaces regardless of the data type

Inheritance: ability for one class to contain the same attributes and methods of another class, parent class has properties that get inherited by the child class.

Generation	Description	Example
1st Gen	Opcodes	Binary
2nd Gen	Assembly	Machine Code
3rd Gen	High Level	C, Java
4th Gen	Very High Level	Python, Ruby
5th Gen	Natural	AI Based

Libraries

A programming library refers to a codebase that can be imported which will contain basic or advanced common functions that can be utilized by a programmer without having to write their own version of the function.

Tool sets

There are many tools that software developers utilize, and it is important to ensure that these tool sets are vetted for security. While developers tend to enjoy freedom and like to implement there own tools and solutions, there should be a process to ensure these tools are authorized.

Integrated Development Environment (IDE)

An Integrated Development Environment (IDE) is a coding platform that can be used by programmers, these programs typically will be focused on a specific language and have features such as shortcuts to finish declaration statements, syntax highlighting, build automation tools and a debugger.

Runtime

The period of time in which a program is being executed, this starts when the program is executed and stop when the program is terminated.

Continuous Integration and Continuous Delivery (CI/CD)

Continuous Integration: developers create branches from a main project, and frequently merge the changes to the main branch

Continuous Delivery: all code changes to the main branch are automatically available to update, allows for automating deployment of an application

Security Orchestration, Automation, and Response (SOAR)

A collection of security software solutions that are combined to create a full suite, typically utilizing automation tools and multiple data sources to enhance security operations, vulnerability management and incident response.

Software Configuration Management (SCM)

The process in which changes to software is tracked, this is a subset of configuration management, which follows many of the same principles, but is specific to a software application.

Code repositories

Code repositories allow for groups of
people to work on a single project and will
typically perform version control. This is a
place that code is stored and generally also
contain documentation on the code. It is
important that these code repositories are
secured and access to them is highly
restricted. Code should be separated by modules
and only developers working on the specific
module should be given access.

Application security testing (e.g., Static Application Security Testing (SAST), Dynamic Application Security Testing (DAST))

Static Application Security Testing (SAST):
effectively a white box test, the code is
openly available for review and is examined for
security flaws

Dynamic Application Security Testing (DAST):
effectively a black box test, the code is not
made available, and the program is tested for
security flaws while it is being executed

8.3 Assess the effectiveness of software security

Auditing and logging of changes

Whenever there are changes to software
security the software should be reevaluated and
audited for the types of changes made and to
ensure that it meets that same level of
effectiveness.

Risk analysis and mitigation

The protection of the software
development process should be evaluated for

risk and appropriate steps taken to mitigate any risks. Risks could be firing a developer working on software that contains trade secrets or algorithms, that developer should have already signed an NDA to mitigate the risk of them sharing trade secrets.

8.4 Assess security impact of acquired software

Commercial-off-the-shelf (COTS)

An advantage of COTS is that it can immediately fulfill a business or technical need at a low cost. The downside of COTS is that it can come with vulnerabilities, and some can affect the organization's information systems once installed and used. Vulnerabilities can exist in COTS because the source code is a black box and the best COTS evaluation options often include using the software in the production environment.

According to the United States Computer Emergency Response Team (US-CERT), security concerns of COTS software include the following:

- COTS software is an attractive attack target because of organizational dependency on them as well as their high profile in the marketplace.
- It is difficult to verify the security of COTS products because they are black boxes to their customers.
- The COTS software vendors have limited liability as designated by the end-user license agreement (EULA) that the user must agree with prior to software use.
- COTS is typically designed without consideration for your specific security control requirements. While this is not universally true, COTS products are usually developed to be standalone products.

Open source

There are many benefits to OSS. First, OSS is often free or more affordable than commercial software. Depending on the software, it can also offer flexibility to modify the program source code to meet your needs. Open source is typically supported by an active community of developers. And it's (arguably) secure.

On the other hand, the downsides of OSS include its complexity, the fact that it often requires technical expertise and a thorough evaluation process, and that it is (potentially) insecure. (There are two sides to the security/insecurity argument, each with its own merits.)

Security risks to OSS come in the following forms and should be key factors in your assessment of the OSS:

- Lack of sufficient evaluation
- Spurious open-source code
- Lack of sponsorship
- Vulnerabilities

Third-party

Third parties can often get utilized for development projects in an effort to reduce risk and cost overrun, however there are inherent risks that come with having third party developers such as not being familiar with coding techniques, lack of direct control on project, possible source code leakage, inability to obtain full source code. While this practice can be safe if outlined properly in contracts it is important to be aware of some of the risks mentioned above.

Managed Services

Outsourcing the maintenance of software, this has security implications as a third party would be performing the maintenance development on software that is being utilized by your organization. The organization that is maintaining the software should be assessed for security posture and bound by contractual agreements.

8.5 Define and apply secure coding guidelines and standards

Security weaknesses and vulnerabilities at the source-code level

Software weakness is a bug or flaw error in the software design or code

Injection Flaws: when malicious code is relayed through another program allowing for execution on the target machine

Buffer overflow: when application memory gets overwritten, and allows for instructions to be written in adjacent memory space

Format Strings: when the input string is evaluated by the system as a command

Authentication Errors: when authentication is able to be bypassed or brute forced due to insecure coding practices

Insufficient data validation: when the program does not validate that the input being requested is proper or what the program was looking for

Security of Application Programming Interfaces (APIs)

The nature of Application Programming Interface (APIs) leaves APIs vulnerable for attack, the resources that APIs are allowed to access should be closely monitored and APIs should be thoroughly vetted for security vulnerabilities before

Secure coding practices

While developing a software application there are many tests that should be performed to ensure that secure coding practices are followed, such as input validation, use case testing, secure memory management, this is all · part of the Secure Software Development Life Cycle (SSDLC).

Secure Memory Management: clearing memory when it is allocated and after the program has finished executing.

Secure Software Development Life Cycle (SSDLC): the integration of security into the software development life cycle (SDLC), with the intent to keep security flaws from entering production rather than fixing the flaw later

Software-defined security

When security functions are no longer tied to hardware and become implemented, controlled, and managed by software. Software can implement security controls across a network to detect, isolate and restrict access to devices or users in an automated fashion based on policy.